MARIO MORONI

THE END OF SOCIAL MEDIA

Second edition March 2024

@2024 Mario Moroni

CONTACTS
mario@mariomoroni.it
www.mariomoroni.it

Youcanprint
"The End of Social Media"

Editing: Roberta Giulia Amidani

Graphic Design: Simone Checchia, Giorgia de Giambattista

Blueorange® design

ISBN | 979-12-22773-43-8

To Valentina, the person with whom I'm lucky
enough to raise Francesco. And to Francesco,
the reason I'm writing this book:

May our walks in nature,
far from screens,
far from algorithms,
far from fears,
guide us on our path.

DON'T SKIP
THIS PAGE

#AIfree

Everything that originally follows has been conceived, produced, and formatted by humans (and I think I'm the first colophon to specify this). *The translation was made by AI, first reviewed by Mario and finally edited by the student of Università Cattolica del Sacro Cuore of Brescia.*

#ObsolescenceFree

One of the problems with books is that they're outdated when they're published. **Except for this one**, which will try to resist obsolescence, meaning it will try to break free from the confines of the printed page, at least for a while.

How?

Through a link from which you can access sources, updates, other links, and extra content.

_42

INTRODUCTION

Hi.

I'm Mario Moroni, I live in a watermill, I work as a podcast producer and recorder, and as an event host.[*]
In 2017 my first book came out.[**]

Have you ever noticed how people tag me
depending on how they're feeling about me?

- Mario Moroni, the coffee-break podcaster.
- Mario Moroni, the speaker of...
- But also, Mario Moroni the startupper.

So, Mario Moroni, podcaster, event host, author of...
Speaker, moderator, writer are just words that, however, have very

precise connotations and effects. Each of these labels creates an image, digging inside our memory and once given, it prepares us for a specific perception.

For example, the term *"host"* recalls the stage, microphone, cameras, audience, maybe Pippo Baudo too, while "writer" suggests a sort of a clear image of a guy that our brain recognises as somebody who writes to earn a living, like Calvino or Hemingway.

While, the word "podcaster", if we don't work in the field or are not usual listeners, will produce more vague images *(and, so, outcomes)*:

---

[*] Even if I totally dislike this word, people use it sometimes...

[**] Actually, the second, no, third. Emoticon by choice. The first was By rage and heart and the second was The first step, a mix between photo and, listen up, poetry. Screaming emoticon.

a pair of headphones, maybe a not well-defined recording studio and, perhaps, the drawing of the radio wave of the apps that release podcasts.

In other words, if this label doesn't apply to our routine, our brain struggles in visualising it.

Vice versa, if it is common, the image is clearer. This, however, doesn't mean that it's real. Neither a representation of it: what we see in our head is a super specific prediction, that is, how we'll see while talking about happiness *(in the CLAN chapter)*, only for us.

Calvino was a writer, like Hemingway.

What if I told you Hemingway was a soldier and Calvino a journalist?

After all, Pasolini* wrote so much,
but we remember him as a filmmaker.

------

*   Pierpaolo Pasolini (1922 - 1975) - italian intellectual, poet, film director, writer, actor and playwright.

Lorenzo Cherubini, aka Jovanotti, has been a DJ for many years, Fabio Volo started as a radio host, but also a baker, Mark Fisher was a philosopher and music critic, while Jared Diamond was a physiologist with a passion for ornithology.

Who are we?

So, what defines who we are?

Reversely, what defines who I am?

If this is what I do, it depends on what I'm doing.

Let's take for example my label of "writer." I'm not Calvino, or Hemingway, or even K-Punk[*], and yet, to accomplish each of my daily activities, I write. But before writing for a podcast or an event, I do research, read, and listen to other podcasts, and watch videos, TV series, movies, and documentaries.

The podcast is the tip of the iceberg, as well as the fifteen or sixty minutes on a stage behind a microphone and in front of a hundred/thousand people, online or live.

Research

For example, it took me years of research, writing, rewriting, reading, and listening to get to the publication of my book: hundreds of hours planned in my agenda and/or taken away from my personal life, and hundreds of sources consulted of which perhaps, less than ten percent made it onto the page, in a text that only destroyed one of the many utopias of our time, namely how easy *(and profitable)* it was to create a start-up.

At the time *(we're talking about the very far 2011)*, every book on the market as well as their nice online courses were just preaching how

---

[*]   K-punk is the pseudonym of Mark Fisher who was a British philosopher, sociologist, music critic, blogger and essayist.

easy it was to launch a start-up and thus live like a nabob.

But that wasn't true.

What I had experienced as a startupper and what I knew from friends/fellow adventurers actually was a movie that bore no resemblance to the very dangerous mythology circulating.

Even if it was a phony myth, it was still a myth, and as such it made victims. I was one of them.

So, because a book that said everything opposite to the others was urgently needed, I started writing it in 2011, and in 2017 I found a publisher who brought it to bookstores.

Almost one year after the publication, someone started asking me for a second edition or even for a sequel, but nowadays the situation has not changed: opening a start-up and especially making lots of money out of it is still really hard.
Really really hard.

So no, this book isn't about start-ups because opening one still doesn't mean becoming a millionaire; even bringing home the bacon can be a problem.

The fact is that today we are on the edge of an evolutionary leap, or rather we are in the middle of it: artificial intelligence undermining work, realist capitalism, the chimera of the customer at the centre, isolation and singularity, the gap between the super-rich and everyone else, the "distant" problem of global warming of which, however, we are beginning to feel the effects and from very close by. All this after just getting through two years of enforced isolation and bulletins.

Today, perhaps more than ever, we are surrounded by an army of trolls/chimeras that we, among others, have fed. For this reason, my goal with this book is to analyse some of them, starting with the proclaimed "end of social media."

Fun fact:
the book is called
"The end of social media".

In fact, that's it: social media are over, and long gone.

In this book we'll see how and, more importantly, in what sense they're over, skipping over the chronicle of the respective media, as well as definitions, tricks, targets, tutorials, and singing stuff *(of which the web is already teeming with anyway).*

That's why this book, just so we understand each other from the get-go, is not for figuring out which social media to use for this or that target, at what age, and at what time, nor does it indicate which ones to delete from our smartphones. It serves *(at least I hope it serves)* to understand where we are, how we are, and most importantly how we can be.

It was not written for everyone, nor for one or more *"target audiences,"* but for four specific people -Fabrizio, Lara, Gloria, and Walter - thinking about what these four individuals want, what they read, what they need, and what they want to know.

Fabrizio is in his mid-30s, works as a freelancer, has a YouTube channel, and would like to be a full-time creator, but he hasn't broken through yet.

Lara is 35 years old and uses social media to read and discover new things; she reads and travels often and is so attracted to cryptocurrencies that she's thinking of quitting her permanent job.

Gloria is 20 and a student: she is attracted to digital communication and would like to become a full-time creator. She tried local radio but was not convinced. She prefers social media where she can do what she wants and when she wants. She's looking for a method to have consistency in content production, but all the online courses she's taken weren't so convincing.

Walter is 38 years old and is a craftsman who has managed to turn his passion into a job. He knows he's very lucky also because he's far away from the "world that matters," as he's always being told to internationalise to sell at his best.

And now, somewhere between a trailer and a spoiler, basically the *"4 books"* of *"The End of Social Media"*.

#takeaway

In the first chapter "THE END", we start not from the beginning of each story, but from its ending, explaining at once why I've chosen a flirtatious title. That's the spoiler: there's a countdown and there are the drums of trolls, but the end of social media and the beginning of artificial intelligence is just the moment in which we have to take our responsibilities: being human to survive, work and be happy. Otherwise, everything is over. The end of social media is an opportunity to understand who we are and what we want to do to be happy.

The -38, "The promises" opens with a flashback back to my eighteen-year-old self-entering the dazzling and brand-new world of social media: for him (that is for the myself of some years ago) social media would have thrown us into a more enlightened world, without borders and without wars. They could have been the new politics. They could have made our lives easier and make us earn a lot of money.

-37, "The other side of the moon" is the chronicle announced of the death of the media giants, and this is where we'll explore the how and question the why.

From chapter -36 to -28, we'll see in detail what type of world early adopters thought would be possible to achieve thanks to social media and the one we have instead, talking about money, politics, wars, but also about culture, freedom, love, and ambition.

From -27 we talk about the myth and myths, what they are, how chimeras are born and above all, what they can do to us: the myth of "we are all influencers", that of gurus and startuppers, of the crypto, the baroque language.

The -19 is tough and although the title is a word that does not exist, "capitalysergic", it talks about capitalism and the boomerang caused by the "customer at the centre". The next of the conflict that we are already experiencing.

The -16 questions reality, or rather, as we will see, on how our specific perception of reality constructs our answers and thus happiness and/or its absence.
Then -15 is about how the logic of clan still influences our lives, a long way from when we humans were just the first "naked monkeys" of the planet (chapter -13).

"The singularity" of the -14 speaks of singularity, loneliness, and other conditions to which we struggle to get used.

The -12 is about how we interface with artificial intelligence. Given that they are there. And the -11 about the fact that AIs are frontiers and should be treated as such. While the -10 frames the algorithm, the ultimate one seems destined to lead us to Turing's point, better known as the "singularity".

The -9 is a fairy tale, while the -8 takes it out on the young. No, it doesn't; on the contrary, it gives a quick overview of who stays and who is leaving the social world, but without giving the numbers that would age the book before it was even published; it is the -9 that takes it out on young people, "against youth", to show us see that this is something we have been doing since Babylon the great, and then talk about revolution, about how much we need it, but ouch ouch, also about the fact that to put one together, we are still four things short.

Finally, from -5 onwards, there is a blackboard with some post-its on which we will see some possible ideas to start imagining a new social, much more social than those we are seeing collapse. we are seeing collapse.

Last point: 'the end of social media' is a podcast book', i.e. a text that I have promised to update with new editions that consider what is happening around us. This is the second edition.

the boomerang caused by the "custo
next of the conflict that we are alread
The -16 questions reality,
how our specific perception of realit
and th

1997
† 2023

Are social media really done for?
Bells have been tolling for some time and we can hear the drums approaching. It's not raining yet, but the atmosphere is gloomy, just like it is in the scene which announces the trolls' arrival: while zillion-dollar empires tremble, millions of human beings have ended up unemployed overnight, and as many find themselves teetering on the edge of a cliff.

Thousands of medium-size, small and micro businesses, freelancers, VAT numbers, companies, freelance teams, on-call employees, gig economists, new uniformed slaves and young dreamers read the headlines and think about their bank accounts, their clients, the invoices they won't issue, the bills they have to pay, their families, their rent and their mortgage, the truck they have just bought *(or the one they will not be able to buy)*.

Fabrizio, Lara, Gloria and Walter - the people I'm writing this book for - call me from their towers to know if it's time to close the bridges.

Someone is scared.

If X falls, I'll lose all my twenty-three clients.

If Y closes down, I'm screwed.

Others scan the internet like Columbus in the middle of the ocean, praying to spot any land. They ask me if social media are really collapsing, if we have really reached the word "end". They want to understand whether it's time to run for our lives, and if so, where to.

Given that they MUST necessarily go somewhere, because they don't have a choice - because you must be there, babe, otherwise you don't exist - they ask me, terrified, which place would be more likely to survive an apocalypse which seems inevitable at this point.

Is this the end, then? Period?
Yes, or maybe not, because "end" is a word which changes meaning based on the context and the variables around it. In Italian "end, ending" is "la fine" (feminine). But if we change it to "il fine" (masculine) it means a different thing, which is "goal, purpose". Its meaning changes if we use "fine" as an adjective, which means "thin, refined" like, I don't know, a thin wrist or a refined hearing, or maybe a refined brain. We also attach it to a measure of time: fine giornata (end of the day), fine-turno (end of shift) or just week-end.
It was nice, the weekend. Can you remember it?
"End", we were saying, is an ambiguous word, a bit like the situation we are living in, in an age where changes are so sudden that they manage to shock even us who work with and within social media, but above all, get by on them.

Social media are our grapevine, through which people can find, follow and buy us. We have studied them like we've never studied any other subject in our life and therefore we know them *(or, rather, we think we know them)*, given that they feed us *(or they will, sooner or later)*.

We even live in them: for most of us, our house and our office are not so far from each other anymore. Our private life has blended with our public life into a slop, where time and space are always the same *(that is, they're never enough)*.

Social media feed us. They fill our days *(and our morning and nights)*.
We see them as a tool to reach a public to which we can sell something *(products, services, consultations, voices, faces, dances, opinions etc.)*

To reach means to intercept, and therefore engage and feed that public with contents which are able to create consensus and inspire trust.

In a word: to engage
(which in Italian sounds quite shitty).

And here we have it,
that engagement which originated the GIG economy.

To engage.

TO ENGAGE

"TO ENGAGE":
a friendly verb, isn't it?

Engagement is everything, without engagement there is no consensus, without consensus there is no notoriety, without notoriety there is no shopping cart.

Intriguing that engaged is the same term that in English is used for an official promise to marry somebody, which in Italian is called *"fidanzamento"*, the phase before *"till death do us part"*.

It comes from the Old French "engagier" that is related to commitments, promises and pledges, whose meaning of "to attract and occupy the attention of" dates back to 17th century *(to be pickier, to 1640)*. In this sentence we can begin to see the trawling nets in which we got more or less consciously into: in attracting and occupying there are concepts of conquest and fight, images of moths attracted by light, and in the verb occupy, even the siege. As we used to occupy a city or a state, nowadays we occupy invisible territories armed with consensus *(likes and sharing)* and market share.

So, we use social media as such, in other words as vehicles, which carry our information around from us to someone else that maybe, with any luck, might be willing to put them in the cart and to buy them.

The problem is that, of these means of transport that we believe we drive, we are drivers, passengers and above all fuel.

THE END OF SOCIAL MEDIA AND/OR EVERY VARIATION OF IT CONFUSES US FOR DIFFERENT REASONS THAT

ALL HAVE SOMETHING TO DO WITH THE FUNCTIONING OF OUR BRAIN.

In order to function, I mean to make decisions, our brain needs to understand and it does it always according to what it knows, even when it doesn't know it at all or when, as in this case, the situation is confusing. The core concept is that when our brain finds itself in front of an ambiguous thing, it must disambiguate it, meaning clarifying it.

Our brain has no alternatives: if it wants to choose how to behave it needs familiar references, meaning known ones that it has already experienced and which it digs up precisely from the past. The trouble is that, since it can't get hold of something such new and never happened before from the past *(like the future of social media)*, therefore it makes some comparisons: if this kind of ambiguous thing looks like the other I know, even just a little, then it's fine.

The brain does try to assimilate future to past, and it's exactly the way it makes us experience the so-called emotional occurrences, the very famous and unknown emotions on which the GIG economy circus relies.

The term *"engagement economy"* was used for the first time in 2012 in an article entitled "The engagement economy: how gamification is reshaping business".[1]

The engagement economy has changed market, rules and playing field on the basis of promises that sounded fantastic: continuous conversation, relationship between consumers and brands, shared experiences, quality connections, customised/custom-made contents, etc.

**Except that they weren't promises,
but slogans.**
Propaganda, actually.
A super effective one.

And this beautiful, very beautiful propaganda came as a trap shaped like a funnel, which is large and comfortable at first, but then becomes tighter and tighter. And so it has spread.

To spread, it used us, propagating through contact and, exactly like the Spanish flu of 1917, it did it through airborne transmission.

In a heartbeat, we went from product oriented to customer oriented, skipping from email marketing to proximity marketing, from social marketing to neuromarketing, from content marketing to loyalty marketing, in the middle of the GIG economy.

GIG ECONOMY

The GIG economy sold us the idea that we were on the threshold of a new world, where it should've been possible to "implement ecosystems able to conquer the hearts of the people and to retain them over the years".

Everything seemed nice and, above all, with good intentions. "In the age of the continuous conversation with our customers and consumers, of the personalisation of contents and experiences and of the marketing technology, we need new visions and new values based on trust, attention and emotion".

Trust, attention and emotion: **WOW.**

After decades of misleading advertising and manipulating selling strategies, something good and nice, at last. They told us it was all about a new economic system still built upon exchange but, in this case, the exchange is based on data and it needs engagement in order to exist.

We were told *(and in a while we will find out who)* that the data is what consumers give us to receive not only products and services but also and above all valuable experiences in time. We learnt that engagement is fundamental, because without it, consumers don't trust us and don't give us consent to use their data, data that we need in order to get to know them better and, consequently, to guarantee everyone an unforgettable, significant and rewarding experience.

It's good to know people to give them something unforgettable, significant and rewarding, isn't it?

Of course, it is.

We all know it, even if *(almost)* nobody told us.

he truth is that we convinced ourselves, inebriated by the possibilities that our brain managed to predict on the basis of experiences that we hadn't actually lived yet. And finally, we started to believe it also because, come on, we couldn't act like neo-Luddites, and at the end, it's the progress, babe.

We convinced ourselves

The word "Luddites" comes from a certain Ned Ludd who, in 1779, allegedly crushed a loom and refers to the henchmen of a working class movement of the 19th century that railed against the new mechanical machines, seen as a threat for workers.
So, the term neo-Luddite includes, and this is a hyper-generalization, those who nowadays - from which the prefix neo - are opposed to technological development/progress, but with a pinch of discernment, just as Gavin Muller explains it in TECNOLUDDISMO:[2] "technologies are never neutral and the incentives to automation and the use of machines during the productive process end up establishing new increasingly pervasive and alienating forms of control and work exploitation.

Luddism

Tecnouddismo

Luddites never wanted to do completely without machines, but they wanted to lead the technological development towards a society in which the workers keep their own autonomy and are the masters of their own lives.

Progress doesn't ask for permission, it can't be stopped, nor can it be hindered. Any try to curb it usually ends up being a dead loss and then makes the future generations laugh.

And that's why we started to repeat ourselves that there's nothing wrong in the system we were feeding and that all the anomalies *(such as the sensitive issue of privacy, or the professional instability of thousands of people, or the increase of depression and anxiety)* would clear up, limiting themselves just as it had happened before *(especially in the best utopias)*.

Ok, maybe someone might be afraid of progress, especially those who don't understand it and don't even try to, but progress is so attractive and full of promises that it would be absurd to even just question it.

After all, all innovations created mistrust and a bit of confusion at the beginning. Think about the electrical lighting that lowered the shutters *(la saracinesca, in milanese)* of hundreds of candle factories. Think about digital photography, bye bye Kodak. Or, even before, about cars versus carriages producers. Think about Gutenberg, who retired all those who worked in the publishing industry before printed paper.

People need time to adapt to changes, and adjust little by little what's not working. Politics and institutions follow, but we can't expect them to keep pace, since "high tech is three times faster than common business. And governments are three times slower than common business. Consequently, the gap amounts to 9 times." according to Andy Grove, the CEO of Intel.[3]

Moreover, we know that when a market closes, there is at least another one ready to open, as if to say "when one door closes, another one opens".

That's exactly what happened with the internet before and social media next: if someone did lose his job, someone else found it, or built it.

When asked if the internet and social media improved our world or not, Luca Soffri answers that yes, the world did improve for those "who have the tools to have it improved and to use it in the best possible way".

With the word "tools", Soffri doesn't refer to a classist subdivision between those who have a fast connection and those who don't have a connection at all *(the famous digital gap that exists in any case)*, but to a wider concept of tools, meaning skills and foresight. And I'd also add lightness and common sense.

The common sense and the thoughtlessness needed not to be dragged into the engagement tunnel, those skills able to protect ourselves from stomachache when our podcast doesn't reach the minimum ratings we expected, or if the sharings languish. So that we don't lose our sleep and the will to go out, we don't fall into depression, apathy, cosmic sadness and into wasted hours spent scrolling kittens and dances.

The common sense not to escape social media as if they were

a cage but, at last, to take our responsibilities also and above all in a period of transition as the GIG economy, which is an insatiable and temporary system itself.

In his early days, it's true, we thought that it would be forever, in order to get rid of the responsibility: tools and means *(and, therefore, social media)* were an excuse not to behave like human beings.

Nowadays the end of social media and the beginning of the artificial intelligence era force us to take our responsibilities: being humans to survive, work and be happy. Otherwise everything is over. The end of social media is an opportunity to understand who we are and what we want to do to be happy.

**"Now this is not the end.
It is not even the beginning of the end.
But it is, perhaps, the end of the beginning."**
Churchill

Now that social media have become essential to have a social life and a job, Mario Moroni comes out with a new book titled "The end of social media?" No, thank you, seriously...

To be honest, it is something that publishing nerds call unmarked titles, a signal, in simple terms, just like the famous fool's gold. Usually, when someone chooses an unmarked title for a book, the reader buys it, or he downloads it etcetera, and then, if he wants to know how it ends, he has to read it all.

On the contrary, with this title, I spare you the effort and make it immediately crystal clear:

26

The end of social media is an opportunity to understand what we are and what we want to do to be happy.

How?

By digging deep.

A little of propaganda on the propaganda engagement.[4]

PROMISES

I am eighteen years old, I live in a watermill in the province of Milan, and there is no screen in front of me:

here is a door, or better, there is a gateway.

The walls of my mill and, beyond it, the boundaries of the municipality have dematerialised. The screen is a Stargate that makes me talk to a friend in Berlin. Together, we are planning a super punk concert in a very cool community centre. It is unbelievable that someone like me, just a normal guy of my age, without any connections, is organising such a colossal event. And all this without leaving the mill. The most incredible thing is exactly the fact of being able to reach everything and everyone in one second, or so. I don't know how it happened, but the Stargate is here, before my eyes. And it isn't just because of the concert that my Berlin friend and I organised.

(For the record: sold out).

The concert is the least of the problems: the fact is that what my friend and I are watching, live, is the beginning of a world that has nothing to do with the rest. Outside the mill, there is the province of a city that looks like a hundred thousand other provinces inhabited by people who don't look like us and who don't know us. They are all people who live like inside a hamster wheel and who have no idea of their situation, people who get up, get dressed, go out and do silly jobs to pay for the things that someone else told them to buy, people who, then, go home and go to bed until the next day, ready to start the loop all over again.

Out of here, all over my screen,
everyone is angry and tired.

I see them in their cars, furious at the traffic lights and queuing in the freeway, but I also hear them at home, every time I try to tell my dad about what I found out.

He doesn't believe in the miracle. In fact, he says that first of all it isn't a miracle, and that, anyway, its days are numbered.

"The internet is a bubble,"

he repeats, using the same words as the ones on the news, "you will see, all this will blow over".

It isn't his fault, of course: he's thirty years older than me, so he can't understand. He was born and raised in a very slow world, written by people even older than him. He doesn't know the Internet. He has no idea of the community that is taking root and of the magic it can do, the magic it already does and the magic that will come soon.

The first magic and perhaps the most powerful of all
is that here people help each other.

If you need a doctor you can find him: you write and someone answers you. Maybe the person who answers you isn't the doctor, but someone who knows him. There is no name for this *(yet)*, but in fact it is a word of mouth. From keyboard to keyboard.

It works the same way if you want to repair your motorcycle: you ask and someone will come up and tell you how to do it. Or if you need information and you want it to be truthful. Truthful meaning unfiltered, made of data that hasn't already passed through the media sieve. Newspapers, television and radio never tell you things as they are: they take a fact, they sieve it with the censor board, they knead it and then they tell you about it to take water to someone who pays them's mill.

Basically, everything that comes out of the media is so commercial that it is used to sell you everything.

In other words, a rip-off.

In here, on the other hand, beyond my screen, things are different.

There is no censorship. Because there is no need of it.

If you're clean, what's the point of censorship?

There is no politics, because there are politicians who go on talking about young people even though they are all old.

Here, there are no old people at all.

There is no business, no votes or money at stake.

WHAT WE ARE EXPERIENCING, MY BERLIN FRIEND, ME AND A FEW THOUSAND OTHER GUYS JUST LIKE US,
IS THE DAWN OF A NEW WORLD WHERE

WE WILL WRITE THE RULES.

A world so cool that maybe one day we could even do without rules, because we will have learned to discipline ourselves, just like an evolution, or rather a re-evolution, of the anarchist utopias.

The emerging community, on forums and on chat rooms, will no longer need politics because it will become the new politics: a politics made by real people, and not by old politicians sat on armchairs.

Here we will be able to learn new languages, jargons, codes and algorithms, to discover stories, to listen to the music we like without paying duty to the record companies. We will be able to meet people, find new friends, from Puglia to Tanzania, maybe even meet our true Love.

We will be able to study without teachers who sleep on their desks, show off, bully their students or behave like assholes. Elders who will punish because you don't think like them, or maybe just because you are young and they aren't *(and they have forgotten that they were once young too).*

We may even discover that studying isn't so bloody boring, and since money or connections won't be needed to get into whichever university desired, but we will only a router, it may even be that we will wish to learn so many more new things.

We may find a job that suits us, and even decide to change it. We may earn enough money so that we won't have to be angry and tired, or worried. We will even be able to make a lot of money without cheating.

Here, from my mill in the province of Milan, the world that is opening up before my eighteen-year-old eyes, has no boundaries.

It is so big and powerful that it is not even a world:

it is a new universe.

My Berlin friend, the other early adopters and I - before anyone called us so - we have before our eyes something that we have never seen before. And yet, despite being something new, we can imagine it and see it almost in detail.

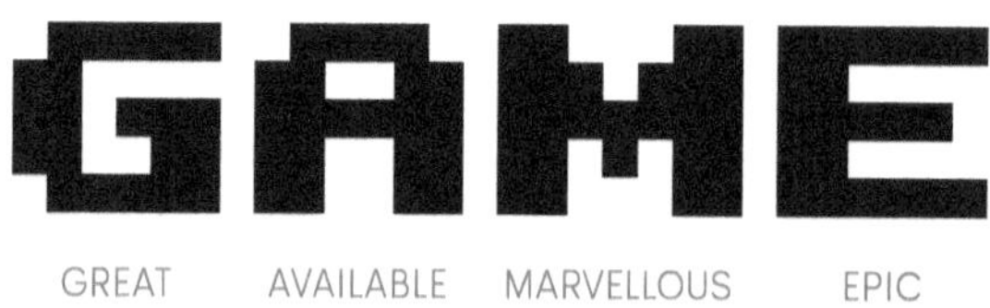

We feel that the revolution we are experiencing will change everything and it will do so for everyone, even for those who don't want to see it, or who reject it because they are terrified of it.

By eliminating distances, we will be able to get in touch with everyone. Without filters and censorship, we will finally have the freedom to express our opinions, and thus to say things as they really are.

This will reduce the power of those who control information, which, in turn, is controlled by politics and money.

new politics: a politics made by real people and not by o
politicians sat on armchairs.

Here we will be able to learn new languages, jargon, codes and algorithms, to discover stories, to listen to the mus we like without paying duty to the record companies. W will be able to meet people, find new friends, from Puglia Tanzania, maybe even meet our true Love.

We will be able to study without teachers who sleep on th desks, show off, bully their students or behave like asshole Elders who will punish because you don't think like them, maybe just because you are young and they aren't *(and have forgotten that they were once young too)*.

As for politics, it will change face too, becoming a popular politics, not made by politicians who are Methuselah's classmates sat on the top of their velvet armchairs, but by the people for the people: the exact opposite of how it works today.

Through the revolution that we are living, it will be us and those like us to change the world, using technology to do good things instead of the usual crap.

Fast forward.
Music:

    Don't Call Me White - NOFX
- What's My Age Again - Blink-182
- Levels - Avicii
- Maneskin :(random pop piece
-

Several years have passed since then, and the world has really changed, but not the way we thought. Some things have changed, such as the economy that triggered a domino effect on people and the planet.

According to some people such changes are irreversible, as Luca Tomassini states, whose mental resources make him see the current revolution as an "evolutionary leap of extraordinary scope" that is not only the product of technological innovation, but the result of our efforts as a human race.

"In an infinite fraction of time, the landscape has changed, as well as our habits, the rules of the game, the paradigms. As it usually occurs in the history of the human being, a single event has started a domino of chain effects that are questioning everything we think we know, changing our lives in a permanent and non-reversible way.[5]"

According to David Wallace Wells, columnist of the New York Times, it is worse, far worse than we think it is; as he mentions in the opening of his book, "The Uninhabitable Earth: A Story of the Future". Meanwhile, the gap between the super-rich and the poor has grown *(see below the survival threshold and the limits of over-indebtedness).*
Politics has also changed, also thanks to the social media, deluding us for a while that we were living a new way of thinking and doing politics, so to show us the beast behind it only afterwards.

Wars continue.

As I am writing this book, the number of wars is so high that perhaps it makes little sense to write the exact number, also because it changes constantly. But I'll reveal it to you anyway: if you own the paper version of this book, you should skip to the link of the website to have the current data.

Generally speaking, there are 59 conflicts at the moment, of which 5 are major, 18 significant, and the rest defined as minor. The first are those wars in which more than ten thousand people die every year and at the moment they involve Afghanistan, Myanmar, Yemen, Ethiopia, Ukraine and the Gaza Strip.[6]

In the chapter -28, A WORLD OF WARRIORS, we will try to ask ourselves why, bringing into play a Nobel Prize that writes to a Pfizer testimonial, and a Pulitzer Prize that digs around the origin of weapons, steel and diseases.

Absurdities as well.

We freed ourselves from distances, and instead of winning more freedom, we lost it: either we are connected 24/7, or we are missing out; either we can say our opinion before or together with other users, or we are missing out; either we gain appreciation *(and consents, sharing, likes, etc.)* or we are missing out.

And in the meantime, there's this rumor going around, like Tolkien's troll drums, that social media has come to an end. Let's get a little closer and listen to what this rumor tells us.

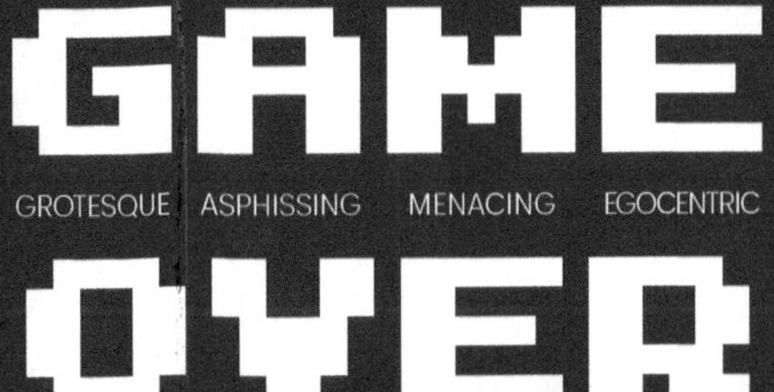
GAME
GROTESQUE   ASPHISSING   MENACING   EGOCENTRIC
OVER

THE OTHER SIDE OF THE MOON

«In the ancient mists of time, in the once glorious days of the former Galactic Empire, life was savage, rugged and fierce, and largely tax-free.»

Douglas Adams

If we believe that every particle in the universe affects every other one, albeit faintly or even indirectly, that every thing is interrelated with all the others, and that the flapping of the wings of a butterfly in China can affect the path of a hurricane in the Atlantic, then the answer to the question of whether or not social networking has reached the end of its universe can only be 42.

42, a four and a two which summed up make six, like the famous six degrees of separation *(which have apparently become five, or rather four).*

42 is an even number, which can be divided into 1, 2, 3, 6, 7, 14, 21 and 42; it's practical, and, among other reasons, it is/it's also the number of imperfection multiplied though by the number of God: 6 x 7 = 42.

That's not enough: Chapter 42 of Lao Tzu's Tao Te Ching gives an explanation of the Universe;
42 is the official distance in kilometres of a marathon, as well as the actual number of images in Carrol's saga Alice in Wonderland, and in the book of dreams *("smorfia")* it's the number of coffee *(Caffettino Podcast!).*

And after some coffee, dulcis in fundo, 42 is the answer Douglas Adams - since we've mentioned him - gives to the basic question about life, the universe and everything, which is the one provided by a supercomputer called Deep Thought after a seven and a half million-year process.

Now that I have recalled why 42 is the answer, let us return for a moment to the flutter of the wings of the butterfly.

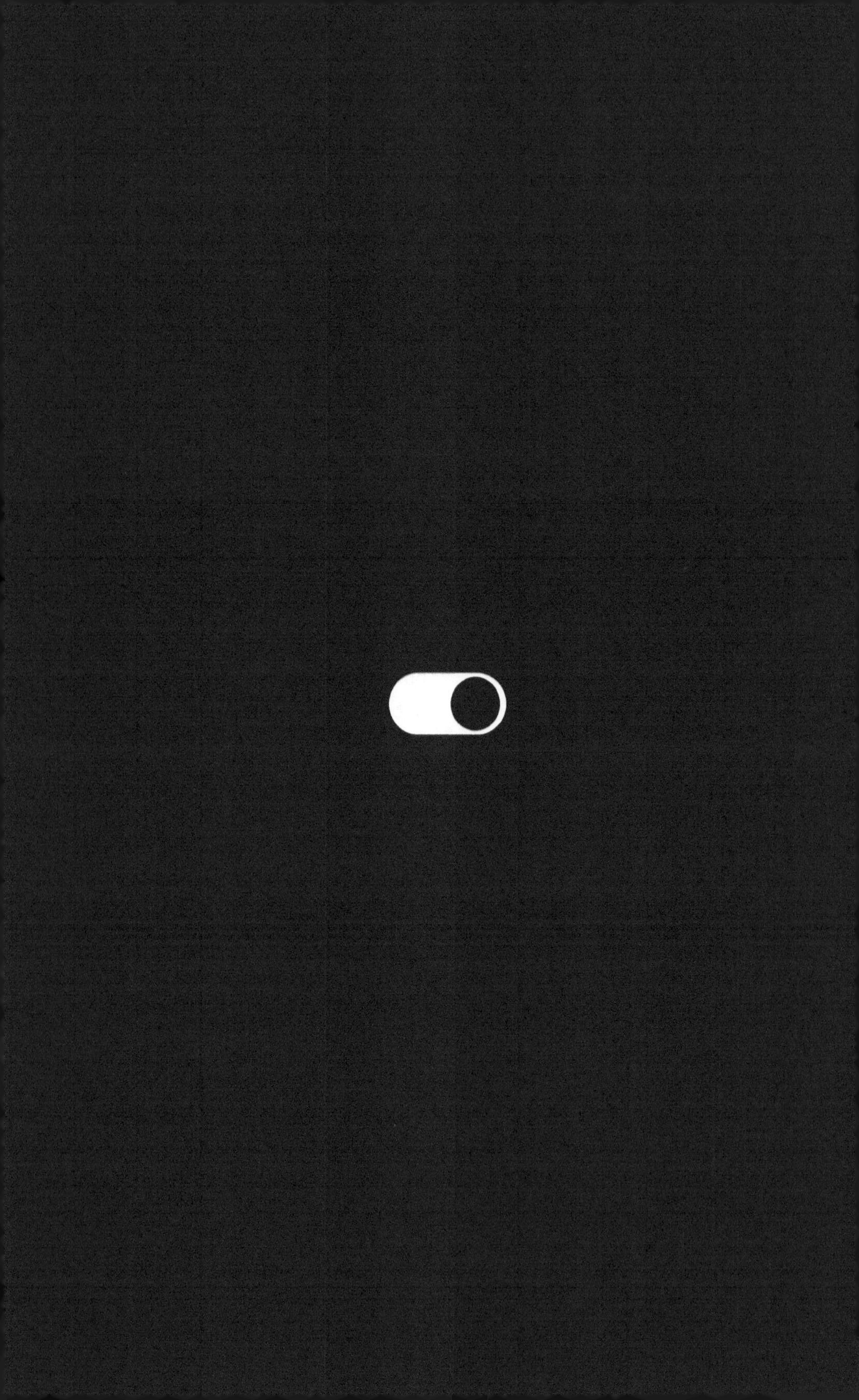

SOCIAL?

During 2022, the stocks of Apple, Microsoft, Alphabet, Amazon, and Meta - the five world's biggest media companies – dropped to double digits, losing between 17% and 67% of their value and consequently making a lot of their investors' money/promising expectations go up in flames[7].

In March 2023, two days after the announcement of the sale of securities for $21 billion, with the expectation of a $2 billion loss, the Silicon Valley Bank shut its doors, kicking off a perfect storm that was amplified by social media and reached Europe, affecting Credit Suisse and Deutsche Bank.

Silicon Valley Bank *(SVB)* was the largest bank in Silicon Valley and the favourite one of nearly half of all the technology start-ups backed by venture capital. Since 2023, it has been a branch of First Citizens Bank, of the Holding Family, North Carolina.

Amidst all this, in front of a few thousand news announcing sickness, carcinosis, death, burial, putrefaction *(etc.)* of social media, there is also someone who argues that they are not collapsing at all, simply because they never existed.

Or maybe they did, but just for a little while, for like five minutes, that is the time *(all)* the young social network founders took to realise that there was something wrong with the system, regardless of all their initial well - very well-meaning intentions.

"THEY MADE THEIR APPS FREE TO GROW THEIR COMMUNITY AND THEN FIGURED OUT THERE WAS NO TURNING BACK. LIMITLESS GROWTH BECAME THE ONLY PRACTICABLE

ROUTE, REGARDLESS OF HOW HOPELESSLY
UNRECOGNISABLE THE PRODUCT HAD TO
BECOME TO REACH IT"

- wrote Ellis Hamburger in The Verge in April 2023[8], revealing how, after seven years working at Snapchat, he had come to discover the truth behind why our most important apps are destined to disappoint us.

Ian Bogost talks about the very same concept in a long article in The Atlantic, [9] which, in extreme synthesis, points the finger at the transformation from social network to social media.

«As its original name suggested, the purpose of social networking was to connect, not to post.»

Except for Twitter, which can be considered the very first real social media, the others were born as social networks, that is to build bridges between people: LinkedIn to find jobs and build nets, Facebook to find again your classmates from university and the fourth cousins who emigrated to New Zealand.

«Then, slowly and shamelessly, social stopped being "networks" and became "media".»

Today we use the two terms as if they were the same thing when they're really not: "A social network is an idle system, a Rolodex* of contacts, a notebook of sales targets, a yearbook of possible soulmates. But social media are active - actually, hyperactive - and spread materials on these nets instead of leaving them alone till you need them."

When they became "highways of constant content**",social media brought both good things and cataclysms.

---

*   Whoever knows what a Rolodex is, put your hand up

**   Ian Bogost, The Age of Social Media Is Ending

› The increasing involvement caused the profits of the ads based on the data of the engagement economy to skyrocket.

› The sudden fame of some people on social media made them precious, therefore creating the myth that started the influencers' circus market.

› Since someone else started gaining by creating content, thousands and thousands of people are now convinced that it's not that hard to become an influencer.

› The platforms *(and not just them)* saw they could gain even from those who were still not gaining but dreamt to, and started selling us the promise we could do it too, obviously with their help, ça va sans saying.

› In the mean time, backstage analysts of these platforms studied the trends, immediately taking the hint that the most emotional content got popular more quickly.

"Polarising, offensive or simply fraudulent information was optimised for the distribution.
When the platforms noticed and the audience rebelled, it was too late to deactivate these feedback circuits."

Due to the financial push from the venture capitalists and from Wall Street, massive growth became imperative, and social networks became social media.

At that point, "the values associated to the scale - reaching a large number of people in an easy and economical way to then profit from it - became interesting to everyone: a journalist and its reputational gain thanks to Twitter; a twenty-year-old looking for sponsorships on Instagram; a dissident spreading their cause through Youtube; an insurrection lover encouraging rebellions on Facebook; a self-pornographer selling sex, or its image, on OnlyFans; a would-be guru selling advice on LinkedIn.*"

So, to sum it all up by the end of the movie, nay, to sum it all up by the end of this first episode of the first season, the very same socials that should have given us a better world actually messed up our lives a bit.

In the next chapters, we'll see how, starting from the world itself, from that small, extremely insignificant green-blue planet, whose life forms, the descendants of the monkeys, are so incredibly primitive they still believe digital wristwatches are an excellent invention.**

---

* Still Ian Bogost, The Age of Social Media Is Ending

** This is still Douglas Adams, the fabulous author of Hitchhiker's Guide to the Galaxy

...AND MEANWHILE PROFESSOR X

HERE IS WHERE WE REVEAL WHERE ELON MUSK'S HIGHLY SECRET PLANS STAND.

Sink

On October 27, 2022, Elon Musk walked through the doors of Twitter with a sink in his hand, and nine months later, on July 26, '23, he changed the name of his new social to X. Over the next twelve months, Musk removed management, initiated a chain of layoffs, and twisted the social's policies, and then reveal X's future with a series of emergency maneuvers. First among them, the fulfillment of his "very secret plan" and that is to make the social platform on a pay-as-you-go basis.

In late October 2023, X shared what was once called a "tweet" that later became a "post," with a fee schedule for new members, on the one hand confirming the cost of the premium version and on the other hand, more importantly, informing users of the mandatory annual fee even for basic functions.

Controversies

The new regulation should serve to *"combat the armies of bots"*[10] and it is already expected to give vent to quite a few controversies around the world, not including EU countries[11] *(and of course China, North Korea, Russia, and various outsiders),* where X may completely disappear.

This was reported by, among many others, Business Insider[12], citing a source close to the company.

Also according to the US news site, *"at the origin of the consideration, there would be dissatisfaction of the billionaire over European regulation of digital services."* And, it also comes to mind, because of problems with the advertising investors *(Musk has lost 59% of sponsors)* who have abandoned him along with, as we have already mentioned, a good part of the users.

Where the former birds have migrated to is soon told: in this respect there is some competition, fresh and varied, waiting at the window. And who knows, it may not be the eve of a Kansas City move, in which an Elon Musk intent on patching up X gets robbed by hordes of users disappointed by new small realities.

Bluesky?

Left rib of the mourned Twitter and which has among its backers even Jack Dorsey, the man who, in 2006, had founded the very Bluebird social network.

SPILL?

Created by two former Twitter employees, most likely fired by Musk. Mastodon? The microblogging social network, that bases its success on the fact that it is free, open-source and therefore the next door neighbour of almost all those disappointed by X.

Or maybe Threads?

When it arrived in Italy, it started with a bang, just like in the United States and the UK, which makes us think that it may follow the same trend: great clamour at the get-go and then less and less, until the end.

Not Meta for sure

even because Zuckerberg in November '23 followed the example of his supreme antagonist by allowing his users to choose between a free and a paid account. The logic: being either your data, or your money. [13]

Meanwhile, with the winter is coming of social networks,

Musk and Zuckerberg are thinking of diversions. An AI doc for businesses for Mark and Elon… *well, Elon has a busy schedule.* After all, the South African PayPal entrepreneur,

father of X, has always diversified.*

His policy is to vary the goals, aim for the most ambitious one possible and accept failure as well as success by moving on to the next goal. Each of his operations has been supported by large impressive communication campaigns, since Elon Musk knows very well how to rally the crowds. Except that the crowds don't always resist his well known, and let's say shaky, coherence.

This is the fault of a rather liberal communicative approach that we could define as "rebounding", due to the incredible peculiarity of reworking opinions according to the "top secret" plan they hide. It happened when he acquired Twitter promising that he would have kept the same name, until he changed his mind and denied everything by doing exactly the opposite. He did it again a few months later, complying with Erdogan's request to block the X accounts of Turkish dissidents on the eve of the state elections, thus betraying the very idea of a social network based on freedom of expression, which had been his slogan from the beginning.

Truth be told, the whole controversial issue of paid blue ticks didn't help Elon's credibility either.

"When he, in March 2023, modified the platform's verification system, allowing users to pay $8 a month to get a blue tick on their profile and to ensure that their posts were given display priority by the algorithm."[14]

---

* In random order, here are some of the latest things Musk has done, straight from his "To Do" list. He launched himself into the space economy by inventing recyclable missiles, made the internet accessible practically everywhere by creating a kind of artificial constellation with Starlink satellites, contributed to the development of artificial intelligence (although he then almost ruined its reputation) and invested in lithium, making life hard for the world's largest car manufacturers with Tesla.

He gave, in fact, the approval to anyone to talk plausible bullshit and then spread it as information of the highest official *(if not ethical)* lineage.

With less than the cost of a pizza and several world-order controversies to sift through, X is flooded with misinformation from all sides.

There are giant chasms in which news thrown to the *(keyboard)* lions as verified sources, including and especially regarding the Israeli-Palestinian conflict, are causing incalculable damage to the already precarious geopolitical balance.

He gave, in fact, the approval to anyone to talk plausible bullshit and then spread it as information of the highest official (if not ethical) lineage.

With less than the cost of a pizza and several world-order controversies to sift through, X is flooded with misinformation from all sides.

There are giant chasms in which news thrown to the (keyboard) lions as verified sources, including and especially regarding the Israeli-Palestinian conflict, are causing incalculable damage to the already precarious geopolitical balance.

Yet, again according to the same NewsGuard survey, "only 79 out of 250 posts containing misinformation about the war had been reported by the platform with a Community Note."

It is in this slapdash manner that Musk's statements often seem to be the result of a hamster on psilocybin. They vary and transform depending on, no one knows what. Moreover, it is unclear how much of this is due to naivety, to pathological loss of common sense or a complete lack of short-term memory.

It would be a bit like promising one's own decisive support to a Country at war and then threatening to take it away, except to offer it again for free. This is something that, in unsuspecting times, Musk did with Ukraine and Starlink.

Always provided that everything is not part of a *"top-secret plan"*, which is what comes to mind regarding his stormy relations with the AI.

Concurrently Musk, with the release of Chat GPT *(of which he is one of the founders)*, stated his concerns about Artificial Intelligence by co-signing an open letter to the world of digital entrepreneurship asking *"to pause for six months the development of AI systems more powerful than Chat GPT4, OpenAI's latest language generator."*

The letter argued that *"AI was advancing too rapidly and unpredictably, risking to eliminate countless workplaces, overwhelming us with misinformation, and even, as a stream of panic-filled headlines pointed out, destroying humanity."*

In short, Musk seemed seriously panicky, but then he corrected his course by switching sides in July 2023, when he announced XAi, his own artificial intelligence start-up. Artificial intelligence for which he promises *(Here we go again Elon!)* hyperbolic capabilities far superior to the competition while staying *"curious and morally free."*

Musk's knockout bombast is in this way: unpredictable. It's capable of sponsoring an aerospace travel company *(SpaceX)* for civilians, giving rise to the tragic narrative of the first humans that could go and die on Mars.

And it makes it impossible to separate the slogan from the truth, the promises from the subsequent haggling. What ever happened, for example, to Neuralink, Musk's neurotechnology company developing implantable neural interfaces, is too early to tell.

For now, things are going great, and after obtaining approval from the Food and Drug administration (FDA) Elon is calling for the first volunteers willing to undergo experimental tests.

One of the noblest aims of the project is to help people affected by quadriplegia due to a vertical spinal cord injury or ALS, to communicate by controlling electronic devices such as computers.

The experimental phase, called Prime (*an acronym for Precise Robotically Implanted Brain-Computer Interface, Bezos has nothing to do with it*) will last six years and aims to verify the functioning of three things together: N1, Neuralink's brain-computer interface, the R1 robot, i.e. the surgical robot that actually implants the device, and the user App, the software that connects to N1 and translates brain signals into computer actions.

Three in One, but Elon won't it be too much?

Not at all.

Should it be successful, Neuralink would mark a grandiose achievement for science and a multi-million dollar success for Musk's pockets, around which, in the meantime, there is no shortage of controversy, such as that surrounding animal testing and the import of pathogens linked to them. But nothing stops Elon from his conviction that progress is in the sign of telepathy, which is necessary to help humans keep up with the rocket-like advancement of artificial intelligence.

A stubbornness that does honour, if nothing else, to the name he cares so much about: X. And which is vaguely reminiscent of a certain Professor X, hero of the Marvel universe: a bald paralytic with a black cat perched on his shoulder who plays at controlling and influencing human minds.

But who is also a natural genius in command of a team of mutants fighting for peace and all gender minorities.

An ambiguous character halfway between a Savior with a far-sighted modern vision and a potential psychopath with a penchant for the limelight.

From the latter perspective, Professor 'Bellicapelli' is a self-centered bastard who plays war with paranormal kids and then sometimes even gets them killed *(when he is not busy lobotomizing their minds)*.

But then again, who am I to say? Truth is in the eye of the beholder.

That is, if they are not blinded by Musk's enormous ego as a luminous sign, as happened to the entire neighborhood of the X headquarters on the 28th of July 2023, when the new logo appeared on the roof of the structure in place of the bird chased from its now illegitimate nest.

A stylistic choice reminiscent of another superhero within the limits of the law. It is a pity that Elon Musk, at least this time, has already turned off the bat signal, leaving his X platform in the dark physically and, considering the balance sheet, also financially.

DUMBO
DUMBO
FRONT&YORK
PARK

CULTURE & WISDOM

Drawbridges

We've just heard of drawbridges ready to close. Here we talk about those bridges that stretch to unite shores and people.

We talk about opened doors, gates and portals. Zeroed distances and crumbled walls, and we talk about #chances, given that we live in the world of possibility, because it is about and it has always been about this: possibility. This is why I'm using the present tense. Every time we came across an innovation, social media included, or rather, every time we imagined one and built it, we did it on the basis of a push towards efficiency.

Efficiency

EFFICIENCY /ef·fi·cien·cy/

Efficiency in a physical-mathematical sense, not a guru-managerial slogan or old-Power Point slide, very dear to consultants.

The push towards efficiency has always been an escape from hassle, because every struggle takes away energy and because every living thing tends naturally to energy-saving behaviours.

› The possibility to do more with less.
Or the possibility to gain the same result, but with less hassle: less effort, less time, fewer costs.

How much?

How much (*sweat, time, lactic acid*) do we need to hoe our six-square-metre vegetable garden with our bare hands?
How much with a wooden stick?
And with a hoe?
And with a motor hoe?

How much time do we need to research something in the only local library, maybe fifty or a hundred kilometres away, by foot or on horseback at most. And how much time do we need if we employ any engine and an AI?

LIFE IS L A Z Y

Potentially, the universe of social media is a portal that breaks down borders, cancelling times and reducing the related costs to peanuts, the exact same Stargate that young Mario Moroni watched while putting up a huge punk concert in Berlin from his watermill near Milan.
The truth is that through social media we could be able to do very useful things, the first of which might be building a better world.

Since "better" is a comparative form, in other words an adjective that compares one thing with another or others, to make sense it needs a context and, of course, a comparison.
The first "better" that comes to my mind is connected to the freedom of learning at *(almost)* no cost, which means more culture and so, maybe, more wisdom.

Any examples?

Learning a language *(including our native one)*, learning to write, read, recycle green onions with permaculture on the balcony.

Learning practical things, from making carbonara to assembling a gazebo; useful activities to feel better, like knowing how our body works, knowing that we are more bacteria than cells, or discovering that our brain is plastic or, even, that every time we drink water from a plastic bottle, some particles of the bottles *(called phthalates)* will remain with us forever.

 ***Phthalates*** are substances that soften plastic, making it more malleable and less difficult to process, but they are dangerous because once absorbed, we cannot get rid of them.

So, theoretically, they are forbidden, but practically, we find them in everything dealing with us and our food *(in food packages, in cling film, in boxes, in water bottles, etc…)*. Not only do they remain forever in our organism, but they also damage our endocrine system by attaching to oestrogen receptors in the brain, messing up the thyroid. If I know what phthalates are, that is thanks to social media, where I got to know a pharmacist who talks about them in her book[15].

57

Among useful and very useful things, learning history through Alessandro Barbero's videos and podcasts. Learning chemistry *(also household chemistry)* to distinguish one detergent from another and maybe avoid the most damaging to us and to our "unimportant, little, blue and green planet".
Learning bad science with Barbascura X.

Understanding something of politics, with Alessandro Masala, creator of the show Breaking Italy.

Discovering or rediscovering philosophy and medicine, being entertained while hearing about stoicism[*], or while watching a surgeon suturing an egg *(Doctor Sutura)*.

But also, finally, starting to see things with different eyes, and more open and finding out that not everybody sees things the same way, and/or that the so-called "diversity" is in the eyes of the beholder, that's what my friend Marina Cuollo recounts on social media[**].

Paying a bit of attention, we could even become more sensitive, which means a bit less obtuse and close-minded, finding out that there is someone who is particularly bothered by special effects, like me or anybody suffering from epilepsy.

Maybe, our applications, filled with UX and UI, are almost non-user-friendly, given the effort we still make to access contents without using hands, eyes or ears. *(And so, we might want to improve them and make them actually user-friendly, not just in words, and thus more accessible).*

Just like, on the other hand, in discovering that there are many of us, I myself could feel a little less lonely and, above all, less different.

---

[*]   Daily stoic has 2 million followers on Instagram.

[**]   Marina Cuollo is also author of "A Disabilandia si tromba", published by Sperling & Kupfer, and of "Viola", edited by Fandango.

A world where the access to knowledge is free is in and on itself a freer world. Given that knowledge is power, a world where learning is possible is clearly better than one where it is not.

The power of learning to do, and then to sell without taking a single step: that is exactly what efficiency is. How cool is it not having to wear suit and tie, to endure x hours driving in traffic to later spend from eight to ten hours in an office?

Who needs a real job?

Only those who do not see that here *(on and with social media)* there is a lot of space, because the engagement economy - "created to give real value and quality contents" - allows us to sell our things all over the world, without moving an inch.

Not being obliged to move means, simply, not needing a motor vehicle and thus spending less for the vehicle at issue as well as causing less pollution. *(Are we sure about it?)*

If people who previously did not have access to knowledge now have it, then the world can only have become better.

However, when we hear about that global warming issue or the fact that phenomena like depression and anxiety are increasing globally, hand in hand with our weight, and one of those few things that are increasing is the over-indebtedness[***], then we cannot but have some doubts.

[***] In simple terms, over-indebtedness, is when our fixed expenses (like mortgage, rent, installments, subscriptions to thousands of platforms, etc...) are higher than our recurring income.

LIKE

Since we have the capability, we should all be less ignorant, even if it doesn't seem like that, so we wonder how good it is what we produce as content creators and what we devour and share as internet users.

Is it entertainment or culture? Is it a way to kill our time or rather a way to waste it? Does it nourish us, or does it drain us?

Let's try to make out what it actually is about by bringing up Pavlov's dog and just a couple of ideas to explain the learning process.

The only possible way to learn is through rewards, that is how every human being has always "learnt how to learn" things.

Pavlov gives Jack a treat while ringing a bell. Jack eats the treat while hearing the sound. Pavlov rings the bell and gives Jack another treat. He then repeats the same action until Jack starts salivating as soon as he hears the bell even when Pavlov runs out of treats.

This system is quite straightforward: when something new doesn't come with a benefit, it will only be perceived as an indifferent "background noise" and we will keep ignoring it; on the other hand, if it does give pleasure we label it as a positive stimulus, a consequence of an even more positive benefit. The more positive benefits are provided by a stimulus, the more we tend to associate it to something pleasing.

On the contrary, if those stimuli lead to unpleasant consequences, we will be drawn to label them as harmful, and this could trigger negative emotions.

So, according to pedagogy and to discoveries on learning and emotions, entertainment itself is a good thing, just

New campaign by the Ministry of Tourism and
Enit conceived by Armando Testa Group[17]

like the ancient Greeks had already understood as they produced theatre plays to promote education within their community. So, according to pedagogy and to discoveries on learning and emotions, entertainment itself is a good thing, just like the ancient Greeks had already understood as they produced theatre plays to promote education within their community.

In his work "Poetics"[16], Aristotle tells us that tragedies started to be staged to evoke sympathy and fear in audiences just to get to the purification of these feelings. Comedy and satire pieces, on the other hand, were aimed to make audiences more aware of their emotions.

What's not so good is the combination between polarisation and the phenomenon of "losing it" we've been experiencing ever since the media understood that content appealing to emotions gets a higher engagement, and we've been exposed to that type of content ever since.

Polarisation ⟶ Getting dumber

Theoretically an incredible enrichment, in practice it has caused a devastating perishing effect. Like the one I get when thinking about the Italian tourism promotional campaign 2023.

This campaign, worth 9 million euros, portrays Botticelli's Venus as a virtual influencer dressed as a biker while enjoying a slice of pizza by the lake, or taking a selfie in St. Mark's Square.

Looking at her I can't help but think of the metanarrative of a stereotypical girl who embraces beauty with photomontages, deepfakes and a deserted uninhabited country. Basically, a selfie in the middle of nowhere.

IIt feels like we went back to 2005, when influencers' stories were considered something innovative and the merging of art and digital still felt fresh and creative.

But "The Birth of Venus" by Botticelli is a painting that represents feminine beauty in art. It's a harmonious and delicate painting. The artist depicts her with a slightly melancholic but serene vein. It has nothing to do with the meta-representation, much less with the stereotype commissioned by the Ministry of Tourism.

At this point, as suggested by many, including my friend Matteo Flora, it was more convenient to create it for pennies with Midjourney and GPT4.

We don't deserve it, because it's a dreary campaign, which shows the gap between the world we could achieve and the one we actually have, instead of displaying Italy for what it really is.

Bye poor
people

Potentially a major enrichment,
turned out to be by far and away a huge fiasco.

We are poorer, or better, #povery *(poor in Italian, but in a social media friendlier version)* in money and ideals.

Instead of getting richer and enriching ourselves, we have been charmed by a very functioning system on paper [vision, community, actual worth for the consumer, moving from the product centricity to the customer centricity, does it ring a bell?] but practically it turns us into rats in a trap.

"Mankind invented the atomic bomb, but no mouse would ever construct a mousetrap", Einstein said, and yet...

The era of

The login era, that is the moment in which we are potentially all connected to one another, is the era of polarisation too, a theme we will soon investigate as we just approach the topic of the algorithm choosing for us.

This is also the "era del rimbambimento" *(in Italian)*, an expression that if it were as close as possible to its Italian original meaning going back to being a child again, it would be great.

Rimbambimento = taking us back to childhood

Unfortunately, it doesn't work like this: as we scroll in a loop for hours, we don't become children again, instead we just get dumber and dumber.

And yet social media should have made us less lonely,

or so they say...

P IS FOR PEOPLE

Here is where we take a quick look at the universe within a click: "If I want, I can speak to anybody."

June, wonderful weather. We're in Cannes, along the Boulevard de la Croisette, in the Palais de Festivals, in a 30.000 m2 area hosting more than eighteen auditoriums. Since 1954 it has been the location of the Cannes Lions International Festival, previously known as Advertising International Festival.

The Cannes Lions International Festival was inspired by Biennale Cinema in Venice, as well as by the "Golden Lion" prize after the lion in San Marco, Venice.

The 57th edition of the Festival, among personalities like Ben Stiller and Yoko Ono, Mark Zuckerberg showed up to receive the "Cannes Lion Media Person of the Year" award. It's 2010, basically the Jurassic era of social media, and only three months before the premiere of his movie "The Social Network" during an interview Zuckerberg talks about relationships, connections and experiences becoming more and more personal.

Connection between people, he says, is the reason why Internet exists.[18]

«I belong to a generation that is different from all the others, the first one to have grown up with Internet. Since I was a child, I got used to seeing new things, interesting technologies. I grew up with Napster, Wikipedia, Aol and everything else. Facebook is the natural consequence because it puts the spotlight back on the reason why Internet came to life, which is connecting people.[19]»

When asked if there ever was a similar moment in history, Mark immediately thinks of the invention of television, but he soon retracts "Tv is a one-way street, while the web offers a brand-new form of participation, it lets you connect with everybody."

CONNECTING PEOPLE is the six degrees of separation theory that becomes more or less "zero degree," as it tears down the distances and especially the differences to even them.

In semiotics, the study of signs and symbols, and in sociology, the six degrees of separation theory hypothesizes that every single person can be connected to any other person or thing through a chain of acquaintances and relations with no more than five elements. The first person to quote this theory was Frigyes Karinthy in a novel that bears his name published in 1929. The first person to put it into practice was the American psychologist Stanley Milgram, who about twenty years later asked 296 people from Midwest to send by post a package to a stranger in Massachusetts of whom they knew the name but not the exact address. In order to do so, Milgram suggested they send the package to the acquaintance that would most likely know the final address, then this person would do the same until the package would actually be sent to the right person.

Milgram thought this process would take at least a hundred exchanges, but the experiment showed that between five and seven were enough.

In 2011 a group of computer scientists from the University of Milan, together with two of Facebook's computer scientists, experimented this theory on a global scale to calculate the degree of separation between all of the couples on Facebook. They found out that, on average, the degree of separation is 4,74.[20]

If we could really get in touch with anyone with less than five exchanges, like it was demonstrated by the experiments, then we are also free to...

The pointer blinks on the page. It appears, disappears, there it is again. The word processor I'm using *(by Larry and Sergey)* shows me a body of text followed by a big and desolated white page. I'm stuck: the amount of things we could potentially do are so massive that not a single one comes to mind.

The pointer is blinking, I stare at it, then the eye wanders upwards, where notifications, that I deactivated, usually pop up, because I have to write 2000 words in the next two hours because after that I have to hurry up and go pick up Francesco from kindergarten.

Time managing needs to be a priority: I learnt that to do what I have to accomplish in the amount of time I have, *(in order to then be free to do the rest)* distractions need to be avoided.

... We are also free to...

Wait. From the top.

What are we free to do thanks to the power of this theory/system of social connections?

› Establish relations that can help us build a network...
No, it's easier! We are free to meet new people *(without moving an inch, so without wasting fuel, time, money, etc.).*

› People that could become an audience for which you can come up with "quality content" in exchange for "engagement"?

› People that could help us, maybe in the role of masters and/or mentors; other human beings who have already done what we want to do and succeeded at it.

> People that could fund our business idea. Business angels, venture capitalists, investors looking for good ideas *(like ours)*. Millionaires who don't know how to invest their money properly.

> People that could become clients?
That means guys that could simply buy our products/services.

> But maybe also people who could become true friends. Or even the love of your life, that is if you haven't met it yet.

If this were the case, out of the blue we should have become less lonely, but we are, more than ever.

We are lonelier now than one hundred years ago, lonelier than we were during the First and Second Industrial Revolutions.
We are lonelier because, way before social media, we abandoned the clan mentality when we left the countryside to move to the city, we've waved goodbye to farmhouses and villages to live in smaller and smaller houses next to factories, next to the teeny tiny studio apartment Pozzetto, which when "Il ragazzo di campagna" (*"The country boy"*) came out it was an exaggeration/a joke, but now it's not that funny anymore.

There you go: folding table, taac... spinny chair, taac... a place for tablemates who aren't there, taac... a metre-long tablecloth, taaac tac, tac tac... Fabriano plate, extra strong napkin, plastic cup, taac... wine in a carton, taac... spaghetti ready to use, frozen side dish, taac... tuna and breadsticks to cut it, taac, tac. Oh yes, that's the life... taac...

Living in a farmhouse was like living in a clan, surrounded by lots of people who were always there and, in all likelihood, also meddling; however, they were also always ready to chat or lend a helping hand when necessary.

70

No babysitters were needed, let alone pet sitters.

The choice of migrating from the countryside was so forced that it was almost not really a choice. It became a necessity for us to move closer to the city so as to get closer to the factories in the suburbs, and in doing so we also came closer to their logic, centred on productivity and product, which was at the basis of Fordist capitalism.

But even after factories and production ceased to be central for many people, their logic has continued to deprive us of two dimensions in one shot. After we got used to having no more space, the mirage of increasing productivity *(an imperative for social media and therefore for us inhabiting them)* has robbed us of our time as well.

I sometimes fall into the trap of doing what I think I should be doing rather than what I want to be doing.

(Bjork)

In the meantime, our village became smaller. The number of children fell also because the very concept of proletariat declined and, due to the stronger desire to climb the ladder in the 1980s and 1990s, the phenomenon of what I call "singularity" emerged *(we will deal with it in Chapter -14).*

71

All couples, including de facto ones, have also diminished.

Divorces have shifted from non-existent/unmentionable to clichés or memes that it is normal to make fun of, and some believe that much of the responsibility lies in the new *(now old)* spaces we live in and the *(few, very few)* people we have around us.

Every five minutes in Italy a couple separates.[21]

Since the introduction of divorce in 1970, the dissolution of marriage has become almost a must, so much so that today almost one in every two marriages ends with a separation.[22]

The first Monday of January has ironically become known around the world as "divorce Monday", meaning the day of the year when most couples reach the breaking point and make the decision to separate.[23]

By 2030, separations worldwide will increase by 78.5% and there will be fewer and fewer children*.

"Less children and more singles" means that our already tiny houses are going to get even smaller following the trends of metropolis like London, Tokyo and Beijing.

Alongside the housing markets *(like the English, Chinese and Brazilian ones)* that are exploring micro modular living solutions, like silos, containers and nano apartments, where eventually we'll take mini appliances and furniture out only when needed and then we'll put them back, exactly like in the film Pozzetto.

Speaking of food, from family pack we now find single servings, designed and packaged for only one person (lonely), on the one

---

*   According to Euromonitoring International esimates.

hand they give us false hopes of not wasting anything, but on the other side – actually – they multiply by ten the waste of plastic, garbage and fuel.

And no, it doesn't cost less, not even in proportion.

If in the farmstead you always found someone to talk to about your spouse, pouring out all your stress to forget it, as well as a grandma to whom you could ask for a recipe or to look after Jack *(Jack the son and/or the Jack Russel)*,

today we are alone.

More than ever.

So no, we are not at all so connected as we could be. The trouble *(another trouble)* is that
we've not become richer yet.

"MONEY"

A RICHER WORLD?
"Get a good job with good pay and you're okay"[24]

Pink Floyd

Money

Money is a recent thing. If we have a look at our time as human beings, even in broad terms, money has been around for five minutes; well, let's make six and a half, if we consider its purpose, that is the mean by which we make possible an exchange between what we have and what we would like to *(and so we include barter)*.

And yet, even if money is something recent, it counts for a lot, since we associate with it the concepts of wealth and poverty that, before being specific conditions, have always indicated someone's status, or rather, something that goes beyond the moment and represents us in front of others.
I said 'always' because, even in the days of our fertile half-moon's ancestors, having more means *(things to trade for more)* was better than having less.

Survival

It's survival, babe: more means, even more camels, equals more chances of having shelter, water and food, even receiving proto-medical care from the village shaman.
Over the millennia, having more means has always meant having a better chance of survival, first and foremost, by eating better.

Medicine

'Let food be your medicine and your medicine be food', read out Hippocrates of Kos, three abundant centuries before Christ, as well as later Galen of Pergamon, the Kneipp abbot of the homonymous path *(1821 – 1897)*, passing through the philosopher Feuerbach *(1804 – 1872)*, who borrowed the phrase from a certain Brillat Savarin - taster and gourmet - wrote 'Der Mensch ist was er isst' which translated stands for 'the man is what he eats'.

Since Feuerbach wrote in German, however, his quote was an overlap between the two verbs (to be and to eat) which in his native language sound almost identical. Having more means really means having access to better food, but not only that: it means having access to knowledge and environments and connections (the famous right knowledge that can help you, find you a job, save your life, etc.).

Besides being the things we eat, we are also the ones we can afford to buy. 'Those seeking wealth are not only looking for oysters, champagne, and luxury jets' writes Giancarlo Orsini in Go, Look at Your Future - 'but above all they are looking for the experience of wealth, that is, the ability to have access to cushy ways of being and living and stop whenever they want.'

Basically, identity.

Through wealth, we dream of being able to buy not only objects, things and houses, Lamborghini and Ferrari, but the fame and notoriety that we envy to super millionaires, whom the Meta tale has turned into living myths. In fact, as we will see in a moment, this new mythology of super millionaires is the 'child' of social media that have sent a handful of individuals to the Olympus of six-figure bank accounts.

People who *(all)* started from a garage and came to build empires listed on the Nasdaq, together with human beings who in the blink of an eye went viral, with a couple of tutorials, or by making fun of those who make tutorials.

MONEY

Delete, ruin, tear, destroy this page.

INVOICE

Ground zero

The ground zero of the other side of the coin is that the myth of this unexpected new prosperity, and no work hard, goes arm in arm with the one of hyper-productivity at all costs that keep us stuck, full time, in the utopian hope of activating the right mechanism to reach the Olympus.

STAND UP AND INVOICE

May I take this opportunity to greet Germano Lanzoni, clapping not only for the #MilaneseImbruttito, but also for all other things he does.

The bacon

Potentially, all this cinema could free up our time and give us a way to become rich and stop worrying about money, and in the meantime make us bring home the bacon.

Meaning: make it to the proverbial end of the month.

First problem

The first problem is that for many of us *(always those on social media)* the end of the month doesn't exist, because we don't have a salary, as a consequence no bank transfer day, only, in case, if everything is fine, invoices to be issued, hoping that we get paid – in the best case scenario – royalties and credits to be collected from Patreon, for example.

Second

problem

The second problem is the downside of the other side of the coin that hasn't two sides anymore but at least three: if we can connect with everyone, then we can also easily make money. If we are not able to make it with all the opportunities we have, even thanks to social media, then we are some pieces of ~~shit,~~ really stinky.

So, a bunch of losers.

79

We are not richer, plus we are not happy at all actually.

Not doing enough to get to the proverbial end of the month, not having enough to fill the gap between us and influencers/billionaires not only means that we didn't make it, but also that we have to sit through the reproach of others, in a society invaded by a collective imaginary that awards the super rich and ignores all the others.

It truly snubs them. The trouble is that super rich people are not many, in fact less and less, while #poorpeople keep increasing.

Martin Wolf, one of the most influential economics commentator, said: "It looks like it's been a long time since the actual economic system produced desirable results for millions of people".

For example, in the United States the income of families barely increased during the last 40 years and young people can't hope to have a more well-off life than their parents: in fact, almost a third of them has seen its own life conditions worsen.
In Italy, where the economic crisis has been even longer and deeper, the available income for families has even moved back."[25]

**If money
buy us happiness
let alone misery.**

Woody Allen

At a certain point from consumers we became prosumers, term that blends together product and consumer.

Mentioned for the first time in a novel *(by the American futurist Alvin Toffler)* of the 70s and then echoed by Philip Kotler at the of the 90s, the concept of prosumer has to do with the customer oriented one, a trap that we'll deal with soon, but that I anticipate/spoiler from the very beginning.
By putting customers at the centre, we have to ask ourselves: at the centre of what? If the customer is at the centre, it means that everything else is not.   Us neither.

So, our devices must be connected 24 hours a day, seven days a week, including, obviously, the weekend, because if the customer - being at the centre - asks, Mario must answer. And it's the same for Fabrizio, Lara, Gloria and Walter.

And everyone else.

It's not enough.

In this new and less rich world, social media serve as accelerators and repeaters, spreading panic, as happened with the Silicon Valley Bank crack.

"This crisis was caused by people on iPhones and other devices, hearing on social media that some bank might be in trouble, " declared Schwarzman, a Bloomberg. "They responded with huge withdrawals in a very short period of time, collapsing the bank".

On the other hand, thanks to all the awareness and the knowledge available to humanity, even if we are *(still)* poor, at least we are not so far away from power and politics as our parents were.

Or are we?

Have social media really become the new politics?
To try to answer that, let's go back to Cannes, back to the 57th edition of the Lions Festival, and listen to Zuckerberg while he says that with social networks 'You also participate in discussions with the government, and this has never happened before.' In his words at the time *(back to 2010)* there are the expectations of all those who believed and, perhaps still believe, that they are at the dawn of a new political system truly based on real people.

That is, from below, from people, and not from the top of some velvet armchair that are geological eras away from real people.

In fact, if politics is the science and art of governing, that is, the theory and practice which have for its object the constitution, the organization, the administration of the state and the direction of public life, then this science and art should really have for its object and interest the public.

In other words, always people, right?

From the Greek dēmokratía, composed of dêmos 'people' and the theme of kratéō 'command'.

Therefore, if people are in charge, people and government should coincide, but this is not the case, since democracy is (or would like to be) a form of government based on popular sovereignty which guarantees to every citizen participation in full equality in the exercise of public power. Which, however, read in this way, says little. To really understand it, you need to grab a shovel and start digging.

If we tear the definition apart, in pole position, we find 'a form of government', which tells us that it is not the only one and that personally makes me want to know how many countries in the world are in a democracy.

The Economist replies: less than half.

"Less than half the world lives in a democracy"

45.7% of the world's population lives in a democracy, full or imperfect, while 17.2% lives in a hybrid regime and 37.1% in an authoritarian regime.

The latest Democracy Index, which measures state's level of democracy, says that only 46% of the world's population lives in a democracy and 'The number is down compared to the year before.'

The Index consists of five indicators: electoral process and pluralism, civil liberties, function of government, political participation and political culture. Each of these indicators is scored from 0 to 10. Then, based on the average, the score is composed to classify nations into four categories: full democracies, imperfect democracies, hybrid regimes and autocratic regimes. This analysis has been conducted annually since 2006, with the exception of 2007 and 2009.[26]

Ranking 167 states,

The Economist then divided them according to scores:

- 21 full democracies
- 53 imperfect democracies
- 34 hybrid regimes
- 59 authoritarian regimes

he most democratic country in the world is Norway, with a score of 9.75. Followed by New Zealand, Finland, Sweden, Iceland, Denmark and Ireland, all with an overall score above 9. Among the large European countries, Germany is in 15th place, the United Kingdom in 18th, France in 22nd and Spain in 24th.

Italy is the 31st democracy in the world and is classified as an 'imperfect democracy'[27], like the United States, which is in 26th place, however. In Asia, only South Korea, Taiwan and Japan are considered complete democracies, while in South America only Uruguay.

Going back to the definition of democracy, the fact that 'It is based on popular sovereignty' could mean that it rests on it. In other words, the aforementioned 'popular sovereignty' is the starting point, not the full picture, while the last part says that *(democracy)* "Guarantees to every citizen the participation in full equality in the exercise of public power."

So, in a way, yes:

social media have become the new politics, and the sense is that they have in fact changed it, so much so that there are those who fear that, unless "We radically change our course, democracy will join feudalism, supreme monarchies and communism as another political experiment that has quietly disappeared"[28].

According to Moore, in Democracy Hacked[29], for example, it is our last chance: "If we don't change the system now, we may not get another chance".

Therefore, the moment seems very critical, as the British Caroline Bassett wrote in Anticomputing published in 2021: "These are the days of politics dominated by Trump's tweets and Russian interference, by the populism of Brexit, fake news and the growing recognition of the monopoly of platforms. We live beyond the knowledge that the Cambridge Analytica scandal gave us, in an age of systematic data acquisition, concern about screen addiction, trolling, bias, misogyny, addiction and all the rest."

NATURAL BORN

In 2023, thirteen years after The Cannes Lion, Zuckerberg -among others declared the need for privacy and a desire to distance his platform from politics in general, wishing for a return to the living room, as if that would drive out the "politics" that in fact have really entered our homes, passing through the windows.

In social media, which began as networks and then became media, we began to make our voices hard, and from social media we propagated them. On the one hand, it is probably thanks to the social media that the political domination of the Clinton and the Bush have ended in America after more than two decades.

On the other hand, it is on the social media where we have given space to characters like Donald Trump and Bernie Sanders in the USA, Matteo Salvini and Luigi di Maio in Italy, figures that are defined by the American writer Nichola Carr as "natural born troll", and whose respective fortunes are based no longer on image but on Snapchat type of personality, that is one that focuses on viscerality and emotion.

TROLL

Intolerance

From, in and on social media we have seen the emergence and spread of new forms of extremism, intolerance, bigotry, aggression and savagery that have touched every scope of the public sphere.

Narod

Thus, on social media, after more than two centuries, the Russian political and cultural movement that in the 1800s extolled the narod, the people, has returned with the term narodnicestvo, then translated into English "populism".

As originally the narodnicestvo aimed at the emancipation of the peasant masses, to greet the end of tzarist autocracy and give birth to a socialist society, the new populism exalts the broad masses, giving them a voice and demanding power.

Contemporary populism divides political and social reality into two mutually opposing entities: on the one side there are people, the good ones, a kind of homogeneous and morally superior entity, and on the other side there are the Elites, the bad ones and great scoundrels who give themselves to take power away from their enemies.

Antipluralists

Populists are always anti-pluralist in addition to being anti-elitist. They claim to be the only ones representing people, even when they push anti-pluralist[30] views, as Nigel Farage who in celebrating the Brexit as "real people's victory" made the 48 percent of the British electorate, which instead didn't want the United Kingdom to leave the European Union at all, a little less true. Or like Donald Trump who – among many (*too many*) horrible things - said in a 2016 rally that "the only important thing is people's unification – because the others don't matter"[31], as if to imply that the only people he deserves is his own, that

is his electors' people, contrasting to the other one, made up by everyone who didn't think like him and therefore "insignificant".

Populists are by self- definition opposed to the national institutions and woe to international heaven *(European Union, Central banks, international monetary fund)*.

They declare themselves opposed to traditional politics, opposed to any tradition except those they choose as belonging to their "affinity group" from time to time, opposed to traditional media as much as they are opposed to new media *(as if there is any difference)*. Since populists are the people, and they are all of them, as if they were cohesive entity, they possess the truth and spread it by raising their voices: they attack, threaten, shout using the semiotics of hate. They prefer writing in capitals because **CAPITALS SHOW UP MORE,**

CAPITALS SHOUT!!!

They use the punctuation to emphasize the affirmations' vehemence. They attack and threaten. In "Ten Arguments for Deleting Your Social Media Accounts Right Now", Jaron Lanier, one of the first who escaped from Silicon Valley – so much as to call himself an apostate – tells us that by encouraging *(or better, even rewarding)* populism, social media have become toxic, and in being that, they are poisoning us.

TOXIC

"Social media is making us sadder, angrier, less empathic, more fearful, more isolated and more tribal."

Lanier

Therefore, social media have actually changed politics, as we have guessed *(and some have seen)* with Salvini's Beast, that is the propaganda machine of the leader of the Lega party Matteo Salvini, which worked for years *(certainly until its creator's resignations Luca Morisi)* thanks to the negative feelings of users on social networks.

The analysis is reported in a study of Pierluigi Vitale, professor of Information design at the University of Salerno and social media analyst, who examined 8.183 of about 9.500 post that have been published between 2015 and 2021 on Salvini's Instagram account, who was at that time minister of the Interior.

The study of Professor Vitale not only tells us that negative emotions encourage engagement, but also that there would be little difference between Salvini's attitude as a minister and that as opposition leader: "after all, if propaganda is the main purpose, whether one governs or opposes, what's really matters is to pull water for their own party's mill".

In order to succeed, the Beast in question, as any others, feeds on strong, or rather fierce content, because the fiercest content travels more and faster, by appealing to emotions, so Lanier explains, as former insider: social media work *(earn money)* thanks to the surveillance and the manipulation of users, rewarding the deepest content because it is faster and stronger:

- surveillance is useful to understand trends
- manipulation is useful to exploit them

TROLL

In this brief description, the trolls, that we have seen in Chapter -41 (the end), return: armies that beat on their drums, annoying the others and encouraging hate, some of them directly "under contract" to politicians.

Politicians on social media need trolls to "attract the distracted attention of millions of potential voters who are glued like zombies to their smartphones, with a communication based on a flurry of messages as refined as machete blows, black or white, strictly without shades of grey, ready to be shared, go viral and be forgotten inevitably. These are the politicians to whom citizens of the social media era want to give their 'like', namely their vote."

The following communication is made up of **UNGRAMAMTICAL SENTENCES WRITEN IN ALCAPS WIT THE URGENCY OF SOMEONE WHO AS TO SHOUT ALL HISANGER AND HAS NOT TIME TO** pay attention to unnecessary things such as punctuation and grammar, a prerogative of elites that they fight and an emblem of the bad guys' superiority they criticize, shoving in their faces that instead of looking for the hair in the egg, they would do better to take care of serious things.

The phenomenon of trolling can be understood as a cultural problem, originating from the techno-social context where we live. It is a reflection of an economic system based on data and engagement, that exalts personal success as the only yardstick and condemns to the media exile everyone who cannot succeed.

In response to the relationship of the people with politics, and of politics with the people, a new kind of "moral panic" is emerging. It crept in and begun to spread around 2011, questioning the *(populist)* form of politicians, of politics, of political life, of public life or of civil society that the societies are letting *(supposedly)* happen by failing to control media.

In other words, we could be facing a new kind of war, new in terms of form and content, according to the drums prophesying its advent.

▶ **Run to the hills** Iron Maiden

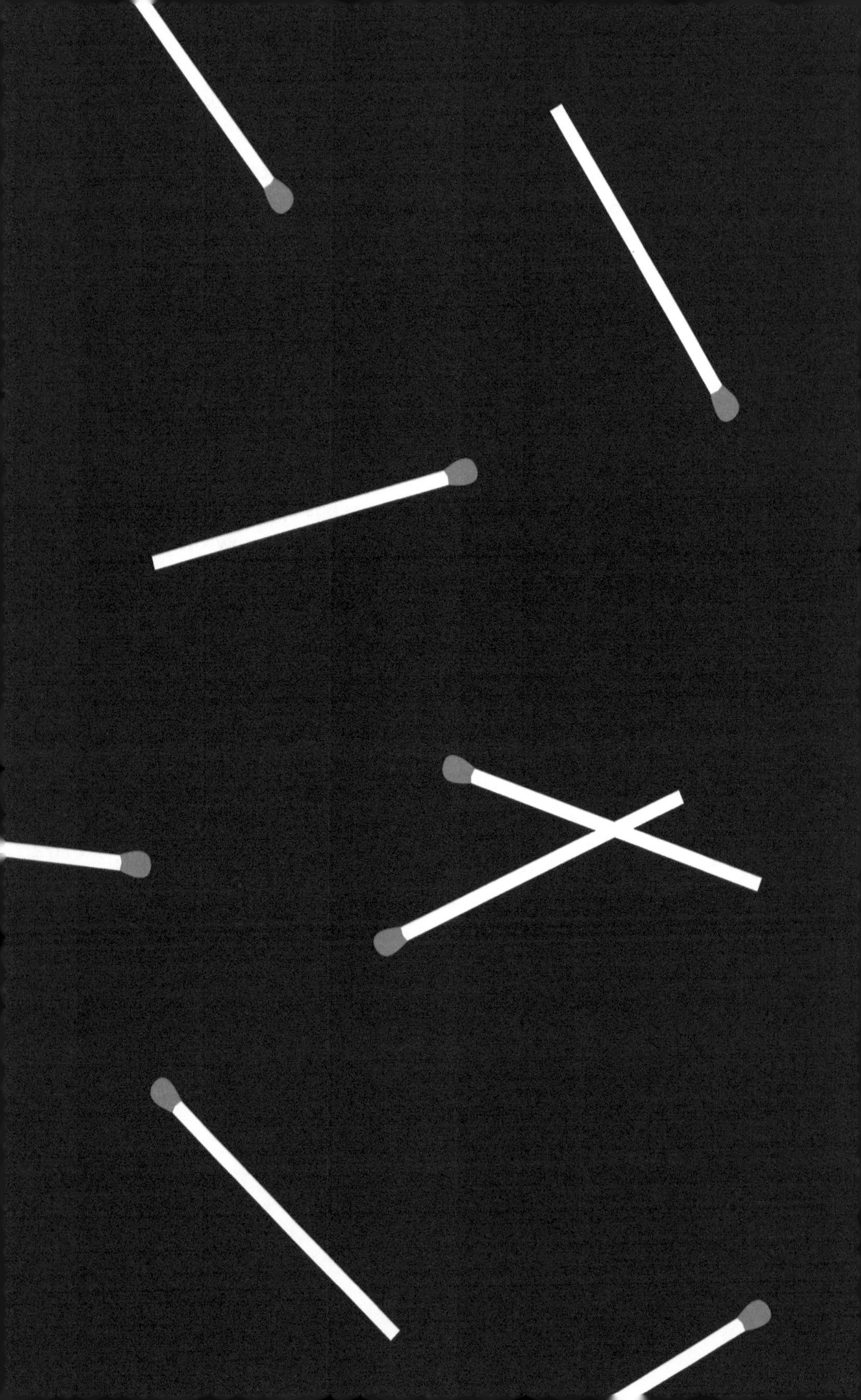

Just right after dawn, we are lying down on a beach facing the Pacific Ocean, on one of the islands of Papua New Guinea, while Yali and Jared are strolling.

Both are in their thirties: the first one is a politician who lives not far away, the second one lives in Boston, Massachusetts, where, among other things, he teaches physiology, although now his interest is not in physiology - which means the study of the vital functions of living organisms, animals and plants - but in ornithology. Basically, he is here [that is "there", unless you find yourself reading me from the same beach facing the Pacific Ocean] watching the birds, so much that Yali is taking him to go around for a walk. As they stroll, the two chat, and at one point, Yali asks Jared why Europeans where the ones who colonized the world.

«But why them?» asks Yali.

Since the first thing that comes to Jared's mind is a strongly racist image that has to deal with the concept of supposed superiority of a certain ethnicity over others, he replies that he must think about it. Hence, he gives him no answer, and continues his walk hoping to spot at least one of the beautiful birds of paradise that the island knows to be populated with.

However, from now on, Jared has a kind of woodpecker that beats him on the frontal cortex hammering him until he pays attention and starts a research that will lead him to publish in 1997 "Guns, Germs, and Steel: The Fates of Human Societies, or Guns, germs and steel: A short history of everyone for the last 13,000 years", almost thirty years after Yali's question. The following year, Guns, Germs and Steel by Jared Diamond **wons the Pulitzer Prize.**

The reason why history has developed in the way we all know is not due to superiority of one species over another, as racists have wanted us to believe for centuries, but due to the geographical characteristics of the territories inhabited by different populations.

Practically, geography and ecology decide the initial advantage of species by giving someone more resources than others: chances to grow roots instead of chasing wild goats and berries, opportunities to stop and study how to heal from diseases, and steel to forge weapons with which to defend themselves and even obtain new territories.

Resources, by getting people's asses in gear, have always moved the world. What resources?
The ones you have and the ones you're looking for.

Niccolò and Matteo Polo in 1266 reached China, arriving in front of Genghis's nephew, Kublai, and a ton of gold, which prompted them to return to Venice and then to organize another trip, in which participated also Marco, Niccolò's son. On the way, Marco sees oil, coal and asbestos for the first time. Once arrived in China, he finds a lot of interesting things (paper and printing, fireworks, matches, porcelain), becomes an officer of the Chinese Empire, and for the next 17 years travels throughout the Far East, from Korea to India.

As soon as he returns to Venice, he writes a book - the Million - which will end up in the hands of the Genoese Cristoforo who reads it and as an antelitteram startupper. He gets financed and sets off looking for the wonders narrated by Marco Polo, arriving in Colombia on 12 October 1492, convinced that he is in India.

Columbus's expedition kicks off the European colonization of the Americas, wiping out entire populations and their ancient cultures.

It is always resources - or rather the growing need for them - that pushes a group of people to wage war on another. Unless you want to believe a certain Mr. Sigmund who in the correspondence with a certain Mr. Albert, a former clerk in the patent office in Bern, blames the early theory of drives.

To open the correspondence in question, dated 1932, it is Albert Einstein who starts like this:

«Dear Mr. Freud,
The proposal, made to me by the League of Nations and its "International Institute of Intellectual Cooperation" in Paris, to invite a person of my liking to a frank exchange of views on any problem chosen by me, offers me the welcome opportunity to dialogue with you about a question that appears, in the present condition of the world, the most urgent of all those posed to civilization. Is there a way to free men from the fatality of war?

It is now well known that, as modern science progresses, answering this question has become a matter of life or death for the civilization we know, and yet, despite all the goodwill, no attempt at a solution has unfortunately led to anything.»

Almost a century has passed since then.

Einstein and Freud are physically dead but continuing to popularize the media. Meanwhile, wars have been started and ended, in chronological order: the Spanish Civil War, the Second World War, the Arab-Israeli conflict, the War of Korea, that of Vietnam, the Six Days, the Kippur, the Iran-Iraq War, that of the Falklands, that of the Gulf, the Yugoslav.

In 2023, there were 59 ongoing conflicts, of which five were defined as "major" (*with more than ten thousand deaths per year*), 18 as "significant", and the rest as "minor"[32]. Among the territories devastated by major conflicts, we include Afghanistan, Myanmar, Yemen, Ethiopia and Ukraine.

Within the subgroup "minor conflicts", from 7 October 2023, that is 50 years after the outbreak of the Arab-Israeli conflict of 1973, we also include the attack of Hamas, and the response of Israel which declared war with a counter-offensive called "Operation Swords of Iron".

Despite being defined as "minor", the conflict resulted in over 8,000 deaths[33], in less than a month since the outbreak, of which more than half were children.

Back some ninety years: Einstein is still writing to Freud and in doing so he plays in advance, hypothesizing that the answer to his question *(is there a way to free men from the fatality of war?)* may lie in the fact that power is in the hands of a minority that has the media at its disposal *(for Albert it was the school and the press, for us it is social media)*, to "organize and divert the feelings of the masses by making them instruments of their own politics".

Freud answers him precisely with the Theory of drives that according to the father of psychoanalysis would be only two species: those that tend to conserve and unite, and those that tend to destroy and kill.

And then he goes on explaining to the physicist already awarded the Nobel Prize *(1921)* that conflicts of interest between men are always decided with the use of violence as happens "throughout the animal kingdom, of which man is unequivocally a part".

In giro che succede
vi faccio vedere come si fa

Santa immaginazione
ho perso le chiavi della città

Magiche le elezioni,
a fare promesse siamo i campioni

Passo l'inverno a tenervi buoni,
cerco l'estate quaggiù in città

E allora sì propaganda, propaganda,
non c'è più niente che mi manca

E allora sì propaganda, propaganda,
la risposta ad ogni tua domanda*

▶ **Propaganda** Fabri Fibra

---

* What's going on around? I'll show you how it goes
Holy imagination, I lost the keys to the city
The elections are magical, we are the champions in making promises
I spend the winter keeping you happy, I look for summer down here in the city
So yes, propaganda, propaganda, there's nothing left that I miss
So yes, propaganda, propaganda, the answer to all of your questions

– Fabri Fibra, Propaganda

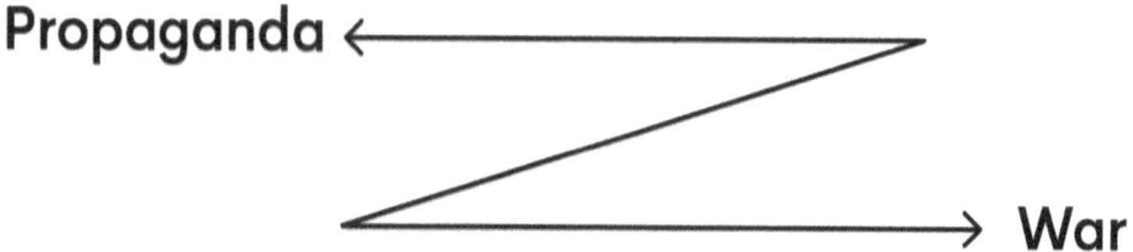

Politics and war are historically linked to the very concept of propaganda (and in that sense to the media that propagate it) and often to fakes: just like Hitler's final solution that originated from an antisemitic fake from the Czarist police – the Protocols of the Elders of Zion – where they claimed that there was an international Jewish plot to take over the world.

Speaking of propaganda and social media, after the 7th of October attack on the Gaza Strip, a parent association in Tel Aviv asked Israeli parents to remove social media apps from their children's phones, "before the militants of Hamas start sharing the videos of hostages taken during the weekend".[34]

What neither Sigmund nor Albert could have imagined was that the media – once completely under the control of a select few – would one day (today) be fueled by the grassroots, that is, by the same pop and populist people we were talking about a few pages ago.
Indeed, the war in Ukraine has been called, if not the first social war, certainly the most viral.

It's not the first one, as social media has become fertile ground not only for people but for communities, state, para-state, private, and illegal organizations.

Some of these territories have proved to be fundamental for social protest movements, such as the 2010 Arab Spring uprisings in Egypt and Tunisia, among the first campaigns in which social media played a key role.
Others have facilitated/are facilitating less enlightened

or even criminal enterprises: for several years, the califate and the Mexican cartels have been using social media to do propaganda and gather proselytes, and Palloywood is the made-in-Palestine video industry that creates content to be shared through social media to push public opinion against Israel. Zelensky is a former comedian[35], as was Beppe Grillo, leader of the Italian Cinque Stelle political movement.

Secret documents

Some secret documents of the US and NATO that contained plans to strengthen the Ukrainian army in preparation for an offensive against Russia were released on Twitter and Telegram in April 2023.[36]

According to an investigation from the Pentagon, the files that were published were allegedly edited in some parts compared to the original version, increasing American estimates of Ukrainian deaths during the war and lowering the number of Russian casualties. This, according to the New York Times, would suggest that the news leak is Moscow's attempt at disinformation.

Interest

Beyond the nefarious use, that is, as a medium that serves interests and/or purposes that are anything but beneficial, social media are certainly capable of capturing the interest of entire communities toward relevant topics.

Too bad that interest fades quickly, immediately replaced by another, as shown by the Arcadia Mood report the year after the Russian invasion.

Analyzing the evolution of content and interactions of Zelensky's profiles and their web clout, the study revealed that after an initial very strong emotional response from users, a sort of quick
addiction to the war took place.

MYTH

If wars continue existing and claiming victims, it doesn't seem like social media have given us a better world or made us *(us users)* better people: they haven't made us more aware, knowledgeable, or empathetic. They haven't made us richer either. They have, however, tricked us into thinking that we can be all those things, someday, if we work hard and commit, posting quality content that will guarantee us the engagement of a zillion followers.

This, at least, they deserve recognition for: they have created a whole new branch of mythology, about modern mythology, made up of the so-called low-intensity myths, as they were called by Giuseppe, aka Peppino, Ortoleva, a scholar of media history and theory, and disseminated by sense-producing machines, as Furio Jesi* alled them as early as the 1970s.

Sense-producing machines or mythological machines are both the process that created the myth - to the point of producing the very idea of myth (*the myth of the myth*) - and the individual sociocultural machines, which produce "materials" or "mythological facts" from time to time in different contexts, and thus also the idea of an instrument of persuasion.

---

*   Furio Jesi was an Italian historian, literary critic, essayist, Germanist and archaeologist, who, for most of his short life (he died at the age of 39 from a carbon monoxide leak coming from the water heater in his home) devoted himself to myth, while also working as a professor of German language and literature at the Università degli Studi di Palermo (without ever having earned a university degree or even a high school diploma). About him - on Wu-Ming foundation - speaks Enrico Manera, Ph.D. in philosophy and teacher of history and philosophy in high schools, who deals with theories of myth and cultural memory in the convergence of history, anthropology and politics. He does so, according to the bibliography at the bottom, citing precisely Furio Jesi: Letteratura e mito [1968] Einaudi, Torino 2002; Mito, ISEDI, Milano 1973; Cultura di destra [1979], Nottetempo, Roma 2011; Materiali mitologici [1979], Einaudi, Torino 2001.

Effects that can be very good, or very very bad, as whenever myth has been used to persuade the masses that a demented idea had a basis, precisely, mythological: the myth of certain "races" being better than others *(and I am not talking about the Samoyedos, although there's something to be said about dogs as well)*, the myth of the conquest *(of the Far West, not to mention the "Italians good people" myth in Ethiopia and Abyssinia)*, the myth of Romanity, of youth, prolificacy and the Mussolini empire.

The same myth that recently turns tyrants into guys who "all in all also did good things." The mythological machine that through advertising has turned a smelly, carcinogenic product into a sex symbol *(tobacco ring a bell?)*, or a medicine that tastes like molasses into the most well-known brand in the world.

Myth, whatever its nature and form, has an extraordinary evocative power: in that it leads us out of the ordinary, to imagine *(see: to evoke, and from evoking to invoking the distance in short)* the grass of the neighbor with an unprecise millions of followers, is already, by definition, greener and richer than our own.

"The press, cinema, widely used literature, ceremonials, the justice, the diplomacy, the conversations, the weather, the crime that is judged, the wedding where we get emotional, our dream kitchen, the dress one wears"; "everything is tributary to the image that middle-class culture makes itself and us of the relations between man and the world," and ends up becoming the norm itself, the model to which individual lives conform to based on certain essential role and status variables.[38]"

"That dreams have power only over your own mind. But with money you can have power over the minds of others.*"

Vikas Swarup

We see a dude on social media. Dude has millions of followers, maybe a gigantic mansion, or a mega yacht, and/or maybe they take a selfie somewhere cool. On their feet are a pair of trainers. No, I stand corrected, only my aunt still calls them "trainers" because the ones dude wears are sneakers, a whole different galaxy. Under the post, a hundred thousand comments tell us that dude is clearly and undeniably happy.

Like us, millions of other people see the dude, and by liking and sharing, the dude's image becomes first viral, then collective, and finally, at some point, the image becomes imaginary and then it becomes a myth that spreads and infects us, contaminating our thought process like a social level, until one day we realize that we need that pair of ~~shoes~~ sneakers because if they are on dude's feet - and dude is a myth – then... - but that's not enough, because in the meantime the same ~~shoes~~ sneakers are on the feet of a hundred thousand other dudes, and from them, even on those of our cooler friends.

---

* "Dreams only have power over your mind. But with money you can have power over other people's minds," from the novel 'Q & A,' by Vikas Swarup, from which The Millionaire (Slumdog Millionaire) movie was later adapted.

With the sneaker example, we're playing it safe: no matter how much the sneakers on dudes' feet may cost, they are just sneakers trainers, and they may even be absurdly priced, but the pricing is limited to the object/symbol. That is, maybe buying the symbol will ruin the rest of our month, but not our life.

The real mess is when the myth makes us want not to wear a part of it, but to replicate its process and fortunes.

"Because if dude made it, then..."

In one word: the status of the myth, which may not even be that big of a deal as a myth, but a little myth, myth-meteor, or a micro-myth.

And here we are, about to stare right into some of these mini-myths: the myth of the influencer, that - again - of the startup, of the high-sounding labels - the "CEOs" et similia - plastered on the profiles of freelancers and slashers, as well as that of a whole generation of self-styled gurus, ready to explain the secret of the world, success, and other wondrous wonders, including crypto.

The idea, as usual, is to dig into ourselves, into the mini myths, to understand where they come from and especially where the heck* they are leading us.

---

* And by the way you can really tell I had a child and matured, right? Back in the Startup days of M I would not have written "damn," but I would have used the most common of synonyms for the male reproductive organ.

Get rid of mini-myths.

Enne is sixteen, he's very handsome and he's never fallen in love with anyone, not even with some Amio, who's ready to do anything for him, including killing himself, running through his own belly with Enne's sword. In fact, he does kill himself, one minute after leaving a message at the Gods' call-centre, so that they avenge such douchebaggery.

Whereas, a few days later, Enne is hanging around in the woods, he ends up lost and starts to call for "help–help" until he meets an unknown girl, a certain E., who, for some old stories I'm not telling you about, can't do anything but repeating what she's just heard.

"Who's there?" he shouts.

"Who's there?" E. echoes.

Although he immediately sends her to ear up, she falls so deeply in love with him that she forgets to eat and drink and, after a very short time, she dies.

At this point, a certain Nemesis, Justice provider for Olimpus joint-stock company, frees herself from her divine commitments and sees to the vengeance implored by Amio, the suicide: while Enne is about to drink from a waterhole, she confuses him so much that when he bends down and sees a face in the abovementioned waterhole, the fool doesn't realise that it is his own face but thinks he has found #truelove at last. The attraction is so intense that Enne stays at the waterhole for hours, then days and finally weeks, staring his #crush as an idiot, and he doesn't do anything else, he doesn't even drink, and of course he doesn't eat. As a result, he dies after a while and, in his place, a white flower sprouts.

But not even death teaches him anything, since during his journey towards hereafter, while crossing the Styx River, he sees the reflection again.

The guy I named Amio is Aminia, while the beautiful E. is Eco and the protagonist Enne is Narcissus of the myth narrated - among others - by Ovid in the Metamorphosis. He is also the very Narcissus that the collective image of the narcissist is named after. This image derives, firstly, from narcissism in the form hybris (a recurring topic in the Greek tragedy that describes individuals who are so rude and arrogant that they cause catastrophes), then in the form of the onanistic preference of those who - in the name of the "if you want something done, do it yourself" - amuse themselves in solitude, and and finally in the form of object of study in psychoanalysis.

In the age of social media, Narcissus is also one of the incentives the myth of our enne-influencers is based on. Nonetheless, compared to the original one in the Metamorphosis, these influencers no longer mirror in a waterhole, but in their very screen.

Narcissus and our Ennes are alone. But, while the former does everything by himself , even annoyed by the interest of others, the latter exists if and only if there's a public who follows him or her.

It's the public who create the influencer: the crowd of followers and the number of interactions carry out the metamorphosis, turning individuals into celebrities who, as a consequence, attract more audience fueling - for 15 minutes, five weeks or five years - the myth-generating machine.

Since many of the enne-influencers tell their stories as "from rags to riches stories", the same mythological machine triggers the idea that anyone can become a celebrity.

But how does this machine work?

How does the transformation that turns the "enne" in the street into a star with millions of followers happen?
If the caterpillar turns into a butterfly following a routine whose logics and rules are the same for every caterpillar, you become an influencer according to a great number of variables which are only apparently manageable.

Being creators, we know that among these variables our contents are in pole position, as well as the right frequency and time to share them and the territories chosen to do it

The contents must be valuable, which means that they must have the very value which, in that specific moment, our specific followers are interested in buying *(paying in engagement: time, data, likes, comments and sharings).*

As a consequence, there's no need for this value to be absolute, nor to be perceived this way by everyone: it's enough that our specific community, the social group we feel to belong to, likes it. In other words, it's enough that it fancies our affinity group, as the "marketingers" would say, or that it interests the community that we already have or we try to build. If we follow the genesis of the mythology surrounding the influencers, it we dig into its origins, we find the same narration at the basis of another myth, that of the californian-model startups, a topic which I covered in my first book and which I'll soon go back to *(chapter -23).*

Contemporary myths rise from the bottom, sometimes from nothing, often as a joke, and/or turning a random passion into six-zeroes empires.

Just like the myth surrounding Chiara Ferragni.

111

"The Blonde Salad never stops,
 and here's how she's made it to the top.[39]"

"If you've never heard about Chiara Ferragni before, you must have been living on Mars.[40]"

"The 30-year-old Milan native launched her fashion blog, The Blonde Salad, way back in the pre-Instagram days of 2009. By 2015, such was her success that Harvard Business Review ran its first-ever case study on a fashion influencer. Ferragni has her own line of shoes and has collaborated with a myriad of brands ranging from Guess to Gucci.[41]"

"Everything started for Chiara Ferragni with the blog The Blonde Salad, launched in 2009, where Chiara poured herself and especially her passion for fashion. The blog, which Chiara often said was started just for fun, became a huge success. By 2014, she was the first fashion blogger to appear on the cover of Vogue.[42]"

113

WHO IS CHIARA?

Blogger

Although many people consider her an influencer, Chiara Ferragni has been, according to the news and the data, one of the first bloggers in the world to start a business which didn't exist before. Therefore, we should look at her from this point of view, as an entrepreneur, or someone who glimpses a specific opportunity, in a specific moment and in an equally specific market, and who on this opportunity starts a business.

But still, we see her as an influencer.

Perceptions

Our perception of Chiara Ferragni which is, by the way, a case study at the Harvard Business School, makes us see her through two different filters: the farsighted and the nearsighted one. They're both bias: cognitive distortions that show us something that's not real, but through the specific filter of our perception.

In the first case, we see her as an influencer that, yes okey, has done great, but for sure has been lucky.

In the distant 2016, The Guardian already wrote £Maybe the older generations will turn up their nose, convinced that success must come from an evident talent, but more and more often it's the people like Ferragni - who has built her career by posing in sexy mini dresses - to be the #winners."

Luck

"The super manager of nothing that took everything. Also Rai - Influencer, entrepreneur, living brand: she is the unquestioned number 1. She can't present, sing or perform: she is perfect for Sanremo" This is the title of il Giornale dated February 2023[43], on the occasion of Sanremo Festival, signed by Luigi Mascheroni, who uses his sharp pen to pull her apart.

"Chiara Ferragni from Cremona - Turòon, Turàs, Tetàs (an expression which refers to three iconic elements of Cremona's culture: the typical dessert, the bell tower and the abundant breasts of its women) - is untouchable in terms of pure success. Every move in the last few years has been an epic win. Who better than her?*"

Through the second filter, the nearsighted one, we think that if she has made it *(to become the most influential among the influencers in the world)*, we can make it, too, without considering *(or better, ignoring)* that opportunities, moments and markets aren't stable and certain data, but a combination of events and people that change every now and then.

Since we don't consider her an entrepreneur, but a successful influencer, we don't even manage to see her exploits, in other words the risks, the investments and the thousands of hours of hard work that Chiara Ferragni has gone through to *"transform her passion for fashion into an empire"*.

Ferragni might prompt eyerolls from older generations who believe success should flow from a discernible talent. But, increasingly, it's people such as Ferragni – who basically made her career on taking pictures of herself in fetching outfits – who are #winning.

"What do Pope Francis, Chiara Ferragni and a student of Content & Digital Marketing have in common? Easy, they are all influencers". This is the claim of a conference organized by Catholic University at the end of 2017, during which professor Roberto Nelli, lecturer of General Management, celebrated the advent of a new era, the era of influencer marketing. "The figure of the influencer already existed many years before the advent of social networks; but it's only with these tools that the influencer

---

*   Mascheroni again

acquires such unprecedented power and range of communication that today we talk about Influencer Marketing."[44]

After all, "we're all influencers" is also the title of an essay written by Gianpaolo Coletti[**] , published in autumn 2022, which contains " a new map which goes towards - I copy from the back cover- niches of value that participate actively" and rattles off […] "game and conversation dynamics with Twitch, the proposals of co-creation with Roblox, the entertainment and the dedication on vertical video streams with TikTok or Snapchat, the increasing curiosity for the immersive stories of the metaverse and for the decentralized infrastructures of blockchain, the aggregation of Minecraft and Fortnite tribes, the boom of the creator economy among all the generations."

As Coletti and others before him said, according to the myth of the influencer, we would live in a world where "a 7-year-old child can change the productive lines of an international giant like LEGO with a letter" and all this because of the magic of the widespread publishing power: "thanks to technology (and to some spirit of initiative) we can all be content creators and gain the attention of a public".

Technology is not only a means, but it's the kind of magic, - as Coletti tells us - which can give everyone, including ourselves the readers, the chance to become

a) content creators

and

b) public conquistadors

It's a pity it isn't true, or at least not anymore. And if we think better about that, it wasn't true even when the book was published, which is inevitable for any book that talks about the present, since it enters the library after being written.

Apart from this one.

** Giampaolo Coletti is a professional journalist and author of different books on business culture and technology, he writes about marketing and innovation for Il Sole24 Ore. He is also the director of StartupItalia and administrator of StartupItalia Open Summit, organized with Bocconi University.

The same happens with research and statistics that portray a very precise moment and spread it - if it goes well - the following year, as the UPA's Surveys (Associated Advertisement Users*), spread in the autumn of 2022, which showed a still very bright picture.

"Influencer marketing enters by right the companies' strategies and budgets, as the increasing investments on this lever of communication say. This year, Italy's expenditure will reach €294 million, 8% more than in 2021; last year it reached €272 million with a 12% increase compared to 2020." Pity that they're surveys *(and their relevance to reality always depends on how questions are placed)* and already old even before being published.

Meanwhile, while social media have entered a crisis and are at a hair's breadth from the abyss, the first inevitable question deriving from the myth *(or better from the cognitive bias behind and inside the myth)* is why struggle if it's enough to post? Why look for a job if I can make millions from my bedroom too?

The second question is how to succeed in it, and it's an issue that, in turn, generates another question: that is the one that platforms answer to by selling techniques and tools, tricks, tutorials, courses and other influencers are ready to reveal the big and dark secret to success.

What if we sold our feet?

If Tom made money by selling photos of his feet, we can do it as well, right?

"From five to a hundred euros for each photo/foot, up to even 20.000 for a shot": here is what we discover if we ask the web.

---

*   UPA is the Italian trade association of advertisers , which are companies that use advertisements to present their products and services to the consumers.

Feet are just feet...
not pornography.

But, even if they were, rumors say that pornography is no longer a taboo, as it's depicted on Money Shot tv series, that frames the history of Pornhub, telling us that the platform has changed the market characteristics, by eliminating the old protagonists from the scene and to replace them with normal people "ready to share imperfect bodies and any kind of fantasies", offering the viewers the feeling that everything is more real".

Then, why not?

... Especially because we use porn as an hashtag: #foodporn for hamburgers, *#bookporn* for books, *#skyporn* for skies, *#snowporn* for snow, *#flowerporn* for flowers and *#travelporn* for pictures of our travels. In my opinion, it's not about what's porn and what's not, or where's the limit we cannot exceed, but where all this can take us to.

That's because, always in my opinion, it could take us to a very bad place.

On average, how much do youtube creators earn?

The amount of money YouTube creators earn can vary greatly and depends on various factors such as the niche, audience size, engagement rate, advertising revenue, and monetization strategies. On average, YouTube creators can earn between $0.01 and $0.03 per view. However, it's important to note that this is an estimate and not a guarantee.

Omg, wtf ? 1–3 cents per view? Can anyone do math?
That means you need 33K — 100K views to make a grand.
I mean, maybe if you have a real cute 5 year old who can open toys on video every day. Exploiting kids on youtube seems to pay well. But otherwise? MY OPINION: OnlyFans prob. pays better for video. #snark #sorry[45]

119

Then, maybe it would be better to follow the example of another category of creators who managed to succeed by selling the tale of how they managed to succeed.

To travel this path, you need a powerful machine *(like a spaceship)* and a lot of fuel.

Some people have achieved this journey,
but the vast majority have not.

They didn't make it not because they lacked the means *(the spaceship)*, but because they lacked the fuel.
Because if the machine *(the spaceship)* is our ability to produce content, the fuel is our ability to attract an audience. And to attract an audience, we need a very powerful fuel.

To travel from the earth to the stars is a very complex journey.

It is not a journey for everyone.

Because if everyone could do it, we would all be influencers. But this is not the case.

The myth of the influencer sells us an easy journey, a journey within everyone's reach, a journey that does not require effort or skills.

A journey that can be achieved with a simple click.

But this is not true.

This is just a myth.

And as every myth, it is not a lie, but a story, a story that tells us something that is not real, but that we would like to be true.

Because we would like to believe that we can become stars with a simple click.

But this is not the case.

The reality is that to become stars, we need to work hard, to invest time and effort, to have skills and talents, to be able to stand out from the crowd, to have something to say and a way to say it.

We need to be able to build a relationship with our audience, to be able to communicate with them, to be able to inspire them, to be able to make them dream.
We need to be authentic, to be genuine, to be true to ourselves.
Because this is what people are looking for, this is what people want to see, this is what people want to follow.

And this is what Chiara Ferragni has done.

She has been able to build a relationship with her audience, she has been able to communicate with them, she has been able to inspire them, she has been able to make them dream.

She has been authentic, she has been genuine, she has been true to herself.

And this is why she has become a star.

Not because of a simple click, but because of her hard work, her talent, her ability to stand out from the crowd, her ability to say something in a unique way.

This is the reality of the influencer.
And this is the reality that we should all aim for, if we want to become stars.

Not the myth, but the reality.

121

LUXURY RECEIPT
DUBAI

RECEIPT: 2942
DATE: 06/05/2023

6	Beef	3000.00
5	Mojito	350.00
3	Negroni	210.00
5	Open food	5000.00
3	Champagne	4200.00

TOTAL   12760.00

TAX ZER0

====================================

THANK YOU
HAVE A NICE DAY

GURU

HERE IT IS WHERE WE TALK ABOUT HOW TO, SELLERS OF READY-TO-DOWNLOAD DREAMS, WOULD-BE GURUS, AND SO FORTH.

When you die, everything will die, except for illumination, your awareness: nobody will ever be able to take it away from you.

Osho

Courses

I start to hold online courses, telling my successful story and I earn millions, or maybe not, not millions, say only the rent, but at least I don't need to work, surely not in an office, since if I can *(and everyone says that you can, don't they?)* make a living, by sharing high-quality contents, well, then that's it.

The point is that *(for now)* I don't have a successful story to tell but, as I was saying, it is a temporary situation. This means, in effect, that it's enough to enter social networks and to show how something at random is done to... let me think about it... to even stop doing it, maybe.

Not bad, right?

Emoticon wearing sunglasses.

If, for example, this something were fitness, it seems it could be enough to create engagement on social media not to worry about going out and reach the three fitness centres where I teach, depending on the hour and the day, crossfit, Calisthenics, Tai-chi and zumba *(a bit out of date, but still popular among a certain type of public)*.

Objects of interest

Moreover, whether the thing/object I'm interested in is finance, trading, real estate speculation or marketing *(preceded by emotional, neuro, engagement, influence etcetera)*, the promises are the same: "follow me and you'll have my secret to...".
That's the claim of hundredthousands of accounts.

In the meantime, enticed by a similar scenario, I study.

Or better, I don't study. because studying is a drag, and not from a drag race, but I watch: I spend entire hours, days and nights scrolling on social media to draw inspiration and, doing it, I find Tom, Dick and Harry who found out how to do it?

To do what?
To create engagement by selling nothing, by only dealing online the recipe of grandma's onion marmalade, the secret to growing an eternal vegetable garden (*I don't know what it is, but we'll think about it*) or even something that sounds super intelligent such as fiscal escapology*.

In the meantime, I've already learnt a trick and precisely from the aforementioned escapology: take any activity and find it a brand name which makes it super serious, better if unclear.

I'm half tempted to go to the neighbour, who has a few hens, and I create an aviantanatotherapy course, presenting it as a new form of rebellion against stress, which has exclusive benefits for those billionaires that a) don't know how a hen is, and above all b) don't know how to spend their billions and are really sad. Nevertheless, my neighbour's hens lay eggs, and anyway I don't want to kill them; so, for this time I pass and keep scrolling.

---

* The original/literal escapology comes from the verb to escape and refers to a form of entertainment in which someone - like Houdini or David Copperfield - frees himself from chains in front of a paying public. On the contrary, the fiscal E. promises to teach us how to pay less taxes, within the limits of the law.

From a content to another one, through several accounts *(of course, and later, in chapter -10 and -8, we'll see why)* I even find a man who explains American people how to speak Italian, and thousands of other men that teach Italian people the English pronunciation, to not mention those who tell me that you can't say "because" they way I say in the province of Milan, but as they say it: with only one e and not thousands of them, and with your mouth shaped as if you were eating a lemon *(by the way, the same mouth that cougars make when they take a selfie)*.

Then, there are those who make tutorials: how to build an emeergency hut in the forest *(I could try in Lambro Park)*, or a gazebo (nice, but I would need at least a balcony), how to make bread and pizza *(but I am on a diet, no bread or pizza)*, or homemade cheese. Or how to lose 7 kilos in 7 days, better if at zero cost and eating like a boar that doesn't move from the sofa. Since I do have a few unwelcome kilos , like everyone, I start right from here. After all, I tell myself in front of hundreds of before-after which are close to science-fiction, if they have made it...

But these are DIY tutorials, *do it yourself,* which my father, and not only him, still calls *fai-da-te*. But as for me, I need something different, which explains to me the method to gain money without working hard.

What do I want?

I want the secret of all secrets.

I want the philosopher's gold of the alchemist told by Walt Disney.

Even more: I want to be Mida.

The king whom Dionysus gives the power to turn absolutely everything he touches into gold, including the soup.

So, I don't need any tutorial, but a #METHOD,

better if a #foolproof one.

On the other side of the screen, hundreds if not thousands of phenomena say that a) it's possible provided that b) you scrupulously and also exclusively follow their Certified and Guaranteed Method by registered trademark, obviously distrusting the imitations of all those wanna-be that mock them. Apparently, you don't need much: you only need to put your email into a form to access contents that each time promise amazing *(and fast, easy and almost without hassle)* results, et voilà, it's a done deal.

Everybody stop now, because here we have another category of tiny-myths, that are those that gravitate around the two-sided coin of methods' pushers, would-be gurus and grand masters of one art or the other.

GUROLOGY

The Guru era started in the USA, conveyed in all in all recent times *(at least on the global time scale, the 80s are recent)* by the giant Antony Robbins, known as Tony, and it spread sailing the ocean as far as the Mediterranean sea's coasts.

"Not everyone in the world is happy, and who is not can drink or maybe rely on personal development, a philosophy of success that combines personal power, positive thought, Self-confidence and the practical manual of the Folletto retailer", Giorgio Viscardini wrote on Vice[46] in 2018. That year the market was worth between ten and fifteen million euros, offering/selling - I quote "everything a man can wish: individual education, aptitude for leading, on-site performances and that thing that anyone, including my cousin that comes from the mountains, has heard of at some point: public speaking". It is an article in which the author gives voice to Roberto Re, Livio Sgarbi and Giovana D'Alessio, three coaches with three very *(very)* different personalities.

The first one has opened the coach era in the Italian peninsula, and the second one has followed in his footsteps declaring to be very happy to be called "guru": both of them sell courses and write best-sellers. While the third one, Giovanna, argues that the improvement method is not purchasable, let alone on Amazon.

The truth is that there is no secret, it's all about marketing marketing, it's all about expedients."

According to Giovanna*, the world focused on the veneration of a winning figure is wrong, just like the culture of contrast in which there are only likes or killer criticism.

Giovanna is a writer too, but her book doesn't deal with self-help, but with a new way of thinking of business organizations. Leaving the physical world to go back to that - equally real - of social media, the myth of the gurus and the coaches, just like the one of the influencers, despite not being evil in itself** produces effects that change our way of thinking and make us believe, on the basis of the luck of few people, that it is possible for anyone - including for ourselves - to become rich and famous without *(almost)* any talent.

---

* AEquacy, to simplify as much as possible, is a kind of organisation without hierarchies already tested by brands such as Nespresso.
** Rather, the principle is excellent, since it's based on the idea that it's always possible to improve ourselves.

Often, the drama is that we are still, with or without social media, in the same morass of that old saying that used to tell : "those who know, do. Those who don't know, teach". A saying that unfortunately has never meant anything, as it was shown by Pfeffer and Sutton* in relation to the "knowing-doing" dilemma.

The knowing-doing gap is the title of the text - published in 2000 - in which the two professors of Stanford University highlighted the detachment between knowledge and actions, in other words, the famous/notorious " it is easier said than done".

Put simply, the knowing-doing gap is the disconnect between knowledge and action. Bottom line, knowing is not always enough. The gap between what we know and what we actually apply in our daily lives is increasing rapidly.

In layman's terms, the difference between knowing and doing is the disconnect between knowledge and action. Essentially, knowing isn't enough.

The gap between what we know and what we actually implement in our daily lives is growing quickly.

"Every year companies spend a fortune on educational programmes, advice and research to enhance their business activity. Nonetheless, the results end up being confined to

---

*   Robert Sutton is a Stanford University professor, chair of innovative management technique with a degree in workplace psychology. Jeffrey Pfeffer is a professor at Graduate School of Business, Stanford University, and author of more than fifteen books translated into many languages.

intelligent discussions and reflections about how you should behave, with modest or no consequences on managers and employees' concrete actions. "

So, it's not enough to know, to do, that is to deliver results. On the contrary and exaggerating, it's not that useful. In fact, the argument is twisted: **who does nothing, knows nothing.**

The (*first*) problem is that if we do nothing, we remain in the cognitive bias of illusions fomented by social media, that attract us towards sellers of ready-to-download dreams . In fact, the mythology implied in the "how to" remains marketable.

How much does TutorMe pay?

TutorMe is an online tutoring platform that offers tutoring services in a variety of subjects to students around the world. According to TutorMe's website, the average hourly rate for tutors is around $18 per hour. However, the actual pay rate for tutors may vary depending on their qualifications, experience, and the demand for their services.

Again, I asked what it pays. On average $18/hour. If you have qualifications. Which means you'd need to do 55 hours of coaching to earn $1000. Course, qualifications might be the sticky part. MY OPINION: Maybe for teachers who get paid crap?[47]

The second one, then, is that those who really make it are very few, it's like saying that there is only one Monty, real entrepreneur of himself who has built a real business and with it he is really feeding many people: not only those who work for and with him, but also the people who, for example, started and restarted reading thanks to his 4books.**

So, as we were saying, in opposition to those few who have made it, all the others are forced to swim in a big, endless and very desolate sea of mud. Just as I said, far back in 2017, with Startup di M.".

**   I guess we'd have to write a book about Marco Montemagno, if he hadn't already.

It seemed easy

They say it's super easy to launch a start-up and get rich as hell. But when I tried starting one myself, I racked my brain for a long time to figure out why I couldn't succeed, to the point of doubting my own intelligence. Maybe I wasn't as clever as my teacher used to say.

Yet I was doing everything right: I worked eighteen hours a day, 24/7, **including mid-August and Christmas.**

Research

But I didn't just stick to work; I also did a lot of research: seminars, big and small courses, and huge conferences, hopping from one event to another looking for knowledge and acquaintances. I put a lot of effort into networking. I met some really knowledgeable people who were super smart and even gave me a hand with it *(some of them became my friends and, after years, we're still tight).*

Tons of books

Meanwhile, I used to buy tons and tons of books about Economics – micro and macro – marketing, neuromarketing, emotional marketing, local and digital marketing, brand identity, IoT, strategy, business, but anthropology, sociology, psychology too, apart from some biographies and, naturally, everything I could find about start-up and Newco.

The funny thing is, I didn't just buy them, I actually read them, some better than others, and more than once; some badly of course, I mean, flipping here and there, often discouraged on the third page.

However, no matter how hard I tried, I couldn't recreate the trivialities I was told, which preached how easy/fast was to start one – even in Italy, in my small village – how to make it work, and how to sell it for millions of dollars. The mainstream narration offered the same four or five common themes, which were also about one single myth. The most common were the garage *(which costs an arm and a leg in the Silicon Valley)*, starting from the ground, the Valley itself, the "fast fail, fast often". The myth *(unique, regardless of the product/service)* was the idea: if you have a good one, then it's done, like those of Jeff, Steve, Sergey and Larry, Mark, etc.

The topoi – that is clichés – and the myth were driven by a super clever mythical machine: even if nine start-ups out of ten ended up failing at the time, people heard about the only one that succeeded. So, the machine started its engine which illuded (myself) to make it and to avoid being one among the discarded.

I really believed it, that I'd make it, to the point of giving up a tough job to open the doors to what I saw as a very bright future *(as a millionaire)*.

I simply hadn't thought about some small things, including perhaps – above all else – that my little country is and always has been wonderful Italy, not the America you often hear about. But it's not just that.

Now, however, since I'm not a fan of people quoting themselves, even in subsequent books, I won't go there. If you are curious about how my adventure started and/or how it all wrapped up, and especially why, I recommend checking out Startup di M.

The bottom line is, whether it's Mario's story or not, the core of this chapter remains unchanged: launching a start-up and ranking in a fortune is still a tough nut to crack, that is, it's not easy, nor fast, nor affordable for everyone. In fact, it costs an arm and a leg.

So, to sum up, if we can't all become influencers, or turn ourselves into six-figure entrepreneurs, or gurus, or make easy money by launching a start-up, at least we still have crypto.

Right?

Let's see.

Puzzled face emoji.

affordable for everyor
arm and a leg.
So, to sum up, if w
influencers, or turn ours
entrepreneurs, or guru
money by launching a
we still have crypto.

Right?

Let's see.

Puzzled face emc

CRYPTO

CRITICS & FANATICS

"If you don't believe it or don't get it, I don't have the time to try to convince you, sorry."

Satoshi Nakamoto

Enthusiasm

From the emergence of Bitcoin onward, the procedure that goes with the innovations has never changed: the enthusiasm of the pro-cryptos versus the envy of the critics.

When it was invented in 2008, Bitcoin worthed less than a penny, in February 2022 a dollar, a few months later 10; in 2013 it was worth already 100 and by the end of 2017, 17,000 and then it fell to 2,500, just to rise up to a bit less than 60,000, by marking the maximum peak and drop again under 30,000.

The highest prize reported by Bitcoin is 59,717.00 Euros.

The lowest is 51,30 Euros BTC.

Skepticals and optimists

Especially at the beginning, as cryptos were emerging and spreading, the number of skepticals was taking over by far the optimists' and few were left to believe that betting on them was worth it. The majority, as usual, was afraid of the unknown, which, however, step by step, started to become less unfamiliar, but was still ambiguous. At that time, these mythological beliefs began to provide expectations revolving around what could easily revolutionise money, payments, finance and everything else.

In this way, the primordial soup of cryptos created *(again)* the idea of us being on the threshold of a new world, and when the crypto's worth started to grow at an unmatched path, the hype sky-rocketed attracting hordes of investors, among which just few owned the resources to invest on it.

While some *(actually few)* have earned fortunes and have told us about them, many have lost every penny, doing the same. Therefore, both fronts have fueled the respective mythological beliefs, contributing to prove the beliefs of the respective groups: whoever would win, strengthened the idea that "you can do it if you want" and the others the idea that "not a chance".

In this picture, - previously described as primordial soup - while the expectations stay the same, the promises have started to totter.

Do we even dare talking about FTX?

It escalated from its collapse *(in November 2022)* to a crisis that has brought million people, and even an entire nation, to their knees.

"The bankruptcy of FTX business, *(in summer 2022)* caused primarily by the actions of its CEO Sam Bankman Fried, is the peak of how the philosophy of effective selflessness is actually a scam in disguise".[48]

"Only after 7 months, the collapse of exchange cryptos has discombobulated the industry that had promised a revolution in the field of finance and has eventually destroyed the credibility of a country."[49]

Speaking of promises, the first has already been broken: technically, by centralising there wouldn't be the need for banking and financial intermediaries, as the Bitcoin Whitepaper premise quoted.

However, it's a shame that Bitcoin basically centralised pretty quickly until it was controlled by a small group of software developers and

Falls

mining pools to function.[50]

In the spring and summer of 2022, various apparently decentralised cryptocurrency operators first stumbled and then fell, bringing to light the fact that they were indeed under intermediaries.

Impacts

Among the negative impacts of the first wave, in parallel with the explosion of ransomware attacks and the suspicion that a financial system based on cryptocurrencies could not be able to solve many problems of traditional finance, we have even witnessed TeraWatts go up in smoke.

> The demand for the power grid of Bitcoin revolves around 138 TWh every year, almost the equivalent of the entire country of Pakistan.[51]

If in 2009 the procedure of Bitcoin mining required only a few seconds of household electricity, whereas in 2023 it required 9 years due to the so called PoW - Proof of Work - which calls for more high-powered computers (*superfast supercomputers, it takes them less to count*) and consequently more energy.

PoW

PoW - as extremely simplified - is a process of trial and error connecting random solutions checking if they are suited to solve computational problems such as the anonymity, Bitcoin authenticity and transaction security in the Bitcoin protocol fueled by the blockchain.

To discourage energy-intensive crypto mining, in March 2023 the USTD released a budgetary framework which calls for a 30% tax on the electricity used by cryptocurrencies miners, triggering a backlash, as revealed by CoinMetrics analysts: "facing that the majority of miners are already squeezed by razor-thin margins, an increase of 30% in their primary operating expenses would be a devastating blow for United States' facilities."

As for Ethereum, the transition from Proof of Work to Proof of Stake at the end of 2022 has decreased the power consumption by more than 99%, as revealed by the Cambridge Blockchain Network Sustainability Index. Since the quantity of energy of a GigaWatt and/or a TeraWatt doesn't ring a bell to many, the index has compared it to some renowned buildings.

If Bitcoins uses as much as Kuala Lumpur's Merdeka, the world's second tallest skyscraper at 678,9 metres, Ethereum has gone from the London-Eye (at 135 metres) which used to serve with the PoW system, to the dimension of a raspberry with the new PoS.

Proof of Stake:

The key players of the PoS are not the miners, but the Validators, who do not need hardwares with high computing power, but rather a network node and tokens to block as collateral. Therefore, the situation has taken a turn for the better, even though the consumption of Ethereum since its founding in 2015 until the transition to the proof-of-stake consensus mechanism at the end of 2022 is equal to that of all of Switzerland in one year.[52]

That's not peanuts.

Beyond the energy issue, which however can't be left aside, it seems that the libertarian myth of cryptocurrency has already started to collapse just like a house of cards, according to what the Italian periodical "L'Internazionale" had already asserted in 2022:[53] "far from competing against the traditional currency, these stocks are purely speculative financial tools and therefore highly sensitive to contingent financial conditions.

Cryptocurrencies do not defend against market manipulations, but they are one of their consequences, especially in a financial system which is drugged by massive central bank liquidity injections *(started in 2008)*.

At this point, one spontaneously wonders whether the system gets drugged just by the previously mentioned liquidity injections, as well as central banks interventions, or whether the problem lies somewhere else and it is perhaps linked to something that in fact ends up drugging also the financial system, something that maybe began way further back.

139

FLUX

A WORLD OF TURGID BUT EMPTY WORDS

IN THIS CHAPTER WE DIG INTO THE LANGUAGE, AND WE TRY TO FIND OUT HOW BAROQUE STYLE NARRATION CHANGES OUR LIVES.

And if it was all our fault?

What if the fault of the ill system we live in *(including the economic and social system as well as the media)* didn't lie on the system itself, but rather on the way the system talks about itself?

What if mainstream narratives were the ones turning potential possibilities into disappointed expectations and a big mess?

Mainstream

This could actually be the case.

Thinking this way would be a form of escaping from our own responsibilities in this world, as we blame something so vague and far from us like the system, which is the result of our communication, figurative and operative choices, which in turn have an impact on communication, the ideas and life of other people. So basically, something that comes from our mind, not an alien virus from Andromeda Galaxy or whatever.

Perhaps, the real alien thing, both literally and figuratively, is another issue related to the concept of "singularity" conceived by Turing

Ambiguity

We must say that the situation is very much ambiguous.

Every time we find ourselves in an ambiguous situation, as we said in the introduction*, iour brain has to simplify it, looking for references from the past and from our imagination in order to make comparisons, but this doesn't always turn out to be accurate *(often making things more difficult for us).*

---

* Perhaps in the first pages of the introduction, but I wouldn't't' put my hand on fire for it

Riding unicorns is way way better.

I think I went through something similar back when I started my first start-up: after reading so many books on how entering this world was all rainbows and unicorns, it was impossible for me to understand what I was getting myself into. And as I could only find those types of books, I didn't realise all of them were actually fiction, and even propaganda to a certain extent, despite them not being considered so.

When I finally started to realise that there must have been something they were hiding and that something was fishy, it was already too late: I had already fallen in the rabbit hole, and I couldn't help but open a start-up myself.

DREAM THE UNICORN
    BELIEVE IT'S A UNICORN
        RIDE THE UNICORN

TELL EVERYONE

After experimenting first-hand and realising I didn't share the same enthusiasm about it, I wrote my first book to show the real truth about this world and I wanted to be loud and clear. I was especially loud in the way I talked about it, also considering the title *(btw it got censored multiple times)*.

It came out spontaneously, with the same tone *(if not harsher)* I used to talk to my public, and years after my book was released, I realised the way I chose to address my readers back then left out a great part of the audience.

Back then I really pondered the choice of using such a low register and slang in my book, but I ended up convincing myself that since that was the only tone of voice my public knew, I couldn't not use it, curse words included.

In this specific book I didn't use any except for a couple *(I may decide to edit them out while revising it, who knows)*, only because, as I got wiser throughout the years, I understood that if my past books were so successful it wasn't because of the type of language I used, but rather because of my critical approach -as many told me- that allows me to dive deep into any topic I discuss to find out what's true and what's fake, and not to be superficial.

All this rambling just to tell you that the words we use
shape our own world.

THE WORDS WE USE SHAPE THE WORLD WE HAVE

They affect it, they change it, they transform it.
They are never just words.

Sorry Shakespeare but you really flopped by making Julliet tell Romeo he could have been named Little Johnny, or that a rose still smells like a rose even if it had another name.

What if a rose
was called cold sore,
would you still think that?

Words aren't just words, they are drafts, shovels and scrapers, bricks with which we can build skyscrapers, or graves, just like drills can dig as deep as the abyss or find oil.
Each word is like charcoal, diamond, or oil from which we

143

get plastic, and our brain is plastic, as well as our emotions that we mould according to what we communicate to our brain.

The narration we expose it to, shapes it into something that makes it *(and thus us)* feel good, better, bad or worse.

Placebo effect, have you ever heard about it?

If we tell our brain that something will benefit it, it will believe it and it will make us feel better, even if that thing is sugar water. The nocebo effect works the same way: if doctors gave us the news that we have a tumour and we had only a few weeks left to live, we would actually die because of that, even if the doctors misdiagnosed the tumour.

Just like when this Clifton Meador doctor misdiagnosed oesophagus cancer (a type of tumour which was extremely lethal back in 1974) to his patient who died shortly after. During his autopsy, it was found that the tumorous cells were only a very few and they were not even detected in that organ.

Since then, over the following 30 years, Doctor Meador started to research the nocebo effect as he felt guilty that someone literally died because of his mistake. "I was certain he had a tumour, he was also convinced he had a tumour, everyone around him was too… Was I perhaps the one who made him hopeless? This case appeared on "Mind over medicine" a Discovery health Channel program (2003).

Words evoke images that each of us elaborate in a different way, in a way that not only changes our world but also the one of people who listen to us, that is to say of those who follow us.

That's why those who address an audience have to be careful not only about what they say, but also how they say it.

RESPONSIBILITY

And since, thanks to the internet and social media, a lot of people do have a voice now, each one of us has a greater responsibility. Brands and influencers also have a greater duty and they can't take a step back, they have to speak up and somehow make it about politics. That's why we need to be careful about the topics we choose to focus on but also the words we use.

On the other hand, some people claim that today there are too many restrictions, and everyone has to be "politically correct" not to be cancelled by haters.

"There are many things in the deep waters; and seas and lands may change. And it is not our part here to take thought only for a season, or for a few lives of Men, or for a passing age of the world. We should seek a final end of this menace, even if we do not hope to make one."

J.R.R. Tolkien

>> *Should we keep our mouths shut?*

Unfortunately, the answer is no, because my co-workers Fabrizio, Lara, Gloria and Walter, and everyone who works with social media, knows that remaining silent isn't an option. You have to voice out your opinion, preferably before others do. That's why it's so important to always be connected and updated.

Freelancers for revenue agencies, subordinate of the system (beehive)*

---

*   The system we live in, the same system Shoshana Zuboff talks so much about in her book "The Age of Surveillance Capitalism".

an endless array of frills
and decorations
that exalt and magnify

BAROQUE
ARRAY OF FRILLS
LANGUAGE
CIRCUMLOCUTIONS
DECORATIONS
PERSPECTIVE
ILLUSIONS

perspective illusions that enlarge,
circumlocutions that take immense detours
and then go nowhere.

The social and social language I see is a language polarised, as we said a few pages ago, and when it is not aggressive, it is still very often exaggerated.

Or inflated or made more complicated/smoky than it needs to be. Basically, baroque language.

When we use difficult words and put it down hard and complicate it, we are not raising the bar, nor are we, but we are only complicating and hardening the overall narrative. According to research - not even that recent[*] - it is now known that often those who speak difficult *(more than is necessary)* do so in order to appear smarter than they are.
More cultured, more powerful. More knowledgeable.

"If you cannot explain something in simple words, maybe you don't understand it."

Albert Einstein

For example, the language of marketing narrative - of slang and acronyms that change all the time - makes it easier for megaconsultants to appear futuristic in the eyes of the eyes of clients who are unlikely to keep up with the latest trends, and thus helps the former to justify the exorbitant fees that the latter are happy to pay and – in in turn - to repeat, certain that naming them will unite them with the ranks of those who know a lot.

Even when they cripple them.

---

[*]   Beautiful and full of insights, in this regard, "The knowing-doing gap" by Sutton and Pfeffer, which we have already mentioned.

Baroque narrative design is also about us, indeed it starts with us: for example, this is the case of certain job descriptions under the name on LinkedIn:

- CEO OF MYSELF
- FORBES UNDER SOMETHING
- TEDX SPEAKER.

Although we would like to think that labels in the manner of the "CEO of myself" are merely the manifestation of a pronounced self-irony, we are in fact feeding - without even realizing it – the mythological machine of success at all costs.

In theory, there is nothing wrong with us telling ourselves how those who have made it, that is, have "turned it around," giving the idea that we are more accomplished, richer, and therefore happier than perhaps we are.
After all, as the Americans say, *"Fake it until you make it."*

We don't hurt anyone, do we? Yes, we do, we hurt a lot of people, the same people who, when reading about us and our success at the head of this or that corporation, will believe in the hot air myth we are selling.

Perhaps, to tone down our language, it would be enough to know that whenever we tell ourselves with lofty titles, we are not so different from Fantozzi's board of directors, such as

Mega

Megadirector Galactic Duke Count Balabam, absolute master of the Megaditta, or Dr. Eng. Grand Mascalzon of Grand Croc. Viscount Cobram, Total Director of the aforementioned.

Dear friends,
the support has changed but
the nameplate is still the same...

director

New word

This chapter's title is a word that doesn't exist in any dictionary: capitalysergic.

From the combination of "capita" + "lysergic", the phenomenon that happens when capitalism becomes lysergic, itself a synergy between narcotic hallucination and lethargy.

Capita is the verb, as is also much of the noun capital, hence capitalism; lysergic is the adjective that describes an acid[*] found in a mushroom from which one can obtain a very powerful hallucinogen like LSD.[**]

Allucinazioni

At the beginning, capital, or rather capitalism, which acts as a narcotic and causes hallucinations, and eventually lethargy. The capitalism we experience today, however, is no longer the industrial capitalism of Marx who portrayed it as a vampire feeding on labour, but - as various currents claim - that of surveillance, which feeds on every aspect of human life, work clearly included.

"We will all work for an intelligent machine,
or it will be that machine that will be used by intelligent people?"

Thus opens the first chapter of "The Age of Surveillance capitalism – the fight for a Human Future at the New Frontier of Power"[***] by Shoshana Zuboff, professor at Harvard Business School since 1981.

---

[*]   "Acid House" by Irvine Welsh must be read, I swear.

[**]   First synthesized in 1938, by Albert Hoffmann, LSD has gone beyond its acid/hallucinogenic status to fuel an entire current of thought, and thus music, literature, cinema, way of living.

[***]   Which the Italian translation published by LUISS, however, softens, removing the word fight from the title.

In this work, already associated with works such as Capital, by Karl Marx, Silent Spring, by Rachel Carson, and '21st Century Capital', by Thomas Piketty, Zuboff explores a recent capitalism, dominated by technology, driven by data and by engagement, which 'appropriates human experience by using it as raw material to be transformed into behavioral data'.

Although this capitalism is dominated by technology, it is not the technology it uses, but the logic that permeates the economy and transforms it into action.

As Zuboff wrote, this is a logic that is not making us richer, as we might expect: 'despite a decade of explosive digital growth, punctuated by the miracle of Apple and the entry of the internet into the everyday life of everyone, due to dangerous social divisions, the future seems to be even more stratified and undemocratic.'

The gap between the super-rich and the super poor is still growing and has done it for several decades now, as already pointed out by the French economist Thomas Piketty, showing that the rate of return on capital tends to exceed the rate of economic growth, and going so far as to suggest that "capital should not be eaten raw".
'Capitalism, like a hamburger, should be cooked by a democratic society and institutions, because raw capitalism is anti-social'.

In which way it is anti-social?

Through inequalities that take us back to capitalism, which Piketty calls neo-feudalism: yet we are no longer illiterate serfs or slaves, right?

The opportunity to have "our lives at an affordable price" has been "the promise at the heart of the digital commerce", from iCosi to the ability to order any product/service at the click of a button, from online learning to the on-demand services of

152

hundreds of companies, apps and web-based devices.

A promise that we liked immediately and still like precisely because it finally understands us and knows what we need.

To achieve this, machine intelligence processes the behavioral surplus by creating predictive products designed to sense what we will feel, think, do now and in the immediate and distant future.

And here, on the aforementioned predictive products, there is another common misunderstanding that leads us (*I'll put myself in the pile)* to think that the media sell data, or process. It to sell it, when in fact, they collect data to sell predictions derived from the collection of behavioral surplus.

The data that the media collects from us serves that purpose: to infer and assume -to imagine and to construct- our specific surplus, which they then sell to those who buy *(and in turn sells)* advertising.

This surplus is not data, nor is it a set of data, but something called UPI, USER PROFILE INFORMATION, and it is not certain, but inferred, assumed, deduced from how we move and behave.

Advertising is the customer, or better who

is always right, by definition.

And even if we keep repeating the thing that says if it is free, we are not the product at all, but the raw material.

"Surveillance capitalism appropriates the. Human. Experience to use it as a raw material to be transformed into data on behavior."

The problem is that to sell advertising, media do not merely observe our behaviors, but create them.
And think about that back in 1999 Google considered the advertising as a "thing of little consequence", so much so

Adwords staff of only four people. A geological eons have passed since then, after realizing the extent of the treasure they were collecting, and after having dealt with a few little problems privacy issues, the media have started defending it 'with their teeth', putting themselves above the law.

"Schmidt, Brin and Page defended with their teeth their right to act without legislative constraints even when Google grew until become the most powerful company in the world".[54]

How come? Simply, in four points that summarized say that the media are so fast that governments cannot keep up, answers always Zuboff.

1. The media are faster and move faster that the state can understand – as Andy Grove said, former CEO of Intel: "high tech goes three times faster than ordinary business. And the governments go three times slower than a common business. Consequently, the gap amounts to nine times".

2. The consequent stupidity and fallacy of any attempt to limit its power.

3. The harmfulness of rules contrary to progress and innovation.

4. The need for the absence of laws to create the right environment for technological innovation.

THE

THE

THEI$

IS

A

R

IS

RI

THE CONFLICT

In all this circus paid by advertisers, at the moment in which we started thinking about the little problem of privacy, and in the meantime becoming annoyed for the invasion of banners and incessant advertisements, it has immediately created a big mess conflict.

Even if social media and the web are so full of advertising to put us off, we can't help it because they are now essential to have a social life and a job.

So, we are all addicted, with the double sense of the term that is both adjective, which distinguishes the addict that lives into us, glued h24 to our screens, and the verb to the past participle of those who depend on someone else, in this case, the media that own the social which invoice converting raw materials (*data on our behaviour*) in predictive products.

But the story doesn't start in the Silicon,
with Steve, Bill, Mark, Sergey and Brin.
It starts before, long before.

It looks like it was an accurate date that messed it all up: 6th October 1979, day in which the Federal Reserve brought the rate of interest to 20%, marking the transition from Fordism to post-Fordism.

Fordism, in two lines, can be summed up in Ford's motto

Any colour the customer wants, as long as it's black.

If Fordism was based on repetitive work that didn't require any qualification and/or specialisation, post-Fordism instead, driven by new technologies, needs specialised and extremely flexible workers.

157

This flexibility was defined by a deregulation of the capital and of the work that led to outsourcing the labour, making work itself less and less stable.

Temps, you know?
**Checco Zalone and
the steady job.**

If in Ford's/fordist assembly line - workers were divided into white-collar and blue-coveralls, separated from one another by walls, and gates, and so unable to talk to each other, - for the simple reason that communication interrupted production - in Post Fordism walls have fallen down because the assembly line has become "flux of information": it is by communicating that people work, and, in this way, work and life become inseparable.

All the italics above is not my doing, but Mark Fisher's, aka K-punk, very brilliant one, in his must-read "Capitalist Realism" who, a few lines later, writes how time is not linear anymore, but chaotic, dot-like.

"To function effectively as a component of just-in-time production you must develop a capacity to respond to unforeseen events, you must learn to live in conditions of total instability, or 'precarity', as the ugly neologism has it."

158

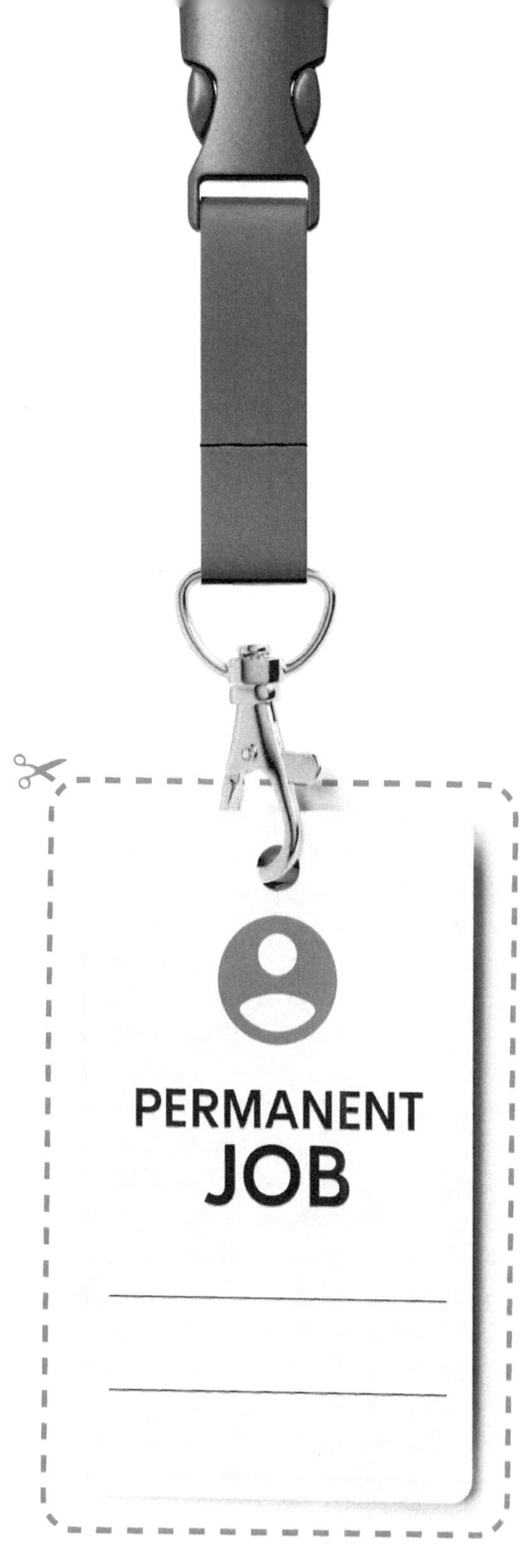

Get your steady job

OH, JIT!

Just in time= always on the ball.

Better if before the others.

Reacting to unexpected events is a thing that anyone who works with/on/in social media knows all too well, just as the matter of time, which is never enough to do everything that we should do, in the ways in which we'd like to do it.

Just in time and gig economy are two faces of the same monster that, by putting the customer at the centre, has gone everything else to the dogs and the monster isn't a dragon, but its handler.
From the "give it to him in any colour as long as black" of the old Henry who brushed aside in a big way his clients, we've reached the growing satisfaction of the customer, risen to the burst that today places *(places us, and places it to us)* at the heart of the whole system.

Let's be clear, it isn't wrong, in itself, to be interested in what the customer wants, what he needs and/or on what makes him more or less happy, but it turns into a disaster when the postulate brings us home the pizza in 15 minutes, with just one click.

Because, if everything revolves around us who are #THECLIENT, like in a Pleistocene commercial of Vodafone, then it has to be made before, and above all, cost less in materials, processing, deliveries, and to be cheaper must pay less who produces, processes, and delivers it.

Talking about pizza, I think of the flour *(I live in a mill, do you remember?)* that, so, must come from a wheat that must grow faster, sprouting several times a year, so with no fear of parasites and bad insect aggression, and therefore requiring more antiparasitic and insecticide.

Wheat must cost less, favouring the biggest farmers as well as the most distant, that live and cultivate lands in states with fewer restrictions about which antiparasitics to use and which not.

At damage of the smallest, those behind the corner, that find themselves crying over spilled milk joining markets in the spirit of zero food miles, whose products though cost so much that they are available just for the elite.

When whole wheat becomes flour, then it gets to the pizza maker who has to work it quickly, reducing the proofing time as well as the other ingredient's quality: he can't prepare the tomato sauce starting from his uncle's tomatoes/those of the farmer, but he needs to buy it from a wholesaler *(coming from)* far far away. The same principle applies to mozzarella, potential artichoke and mushrooms, etc. And for the delivery: the pizza maker can't afford to hire a person *(or two)* to let us get pizza at home in 15 minutes, but he needs to turn to one or more apps, many of which exploited riders*for a very long time.

No contracts, no legal protection:

You made your bed, now lie in it.

The same argument applies to different industries.

Let's think about fashion *(do you remember it?)* with fast-fashion that delivers at our houses or squeezes in shopping centres and hubs, tons of fabric cut and sewed at huge distance from us, often by workers treated like slaves. To reach us and get accumulated in our wardrobes always too full *(or we can't explain the global success of a text, cute indeed, such as "the life-changing magic of tidying up")* it must go beyond those distances, burning down containers of fossil fuel that contaminates our skies and increases the temperatures.

Let's take the music that must be as fast as us, and as us always on the ball.

Let's get closer now. Let's take our jobs as freelance and content creators, that to get going, while we are deceived to be entrepreneurs of ourselves, we are caught in the grips of taxes thought for ATECO (Classification of Economic Activity) categories decades old, Kafkaesque bureaucracy and such schedules that in comparison feudal serfs were doing so well.

But feudal serfs died like flies. They had nothing. And they worked their fingers to the bone from sunrise to sunset, without any protection, let alone contracts.

Instead, we have preventive diagnostics, antibiotics, supplements. We have machines, automation, labour unions *(not us, because we are freelance)...*

At least we don't have to leave our homes to work in fields like our ancestors, factories like our great-grandparents, or offices like our parents.

We tell ourselves that we are free to work from home, except that, actually, our home, the real one, where we live all day long and every day, is social media. Meaning it's the hive Shoshana Zuboff talks about, a space that has pervaded our existence to the point that we can't do without it anymore. If that's how it goes for us that made it our factory, the problem is that's how it goes also and above all for kids, as, already in 2016, said a very happy Michelle Klein, the then Facebook marketing director:

> "While the average adult checks their phone 39 times a day, the average millennial does it more than 157 times."

To the point that we can't do without it anymore?
Worse: to the point that we get sick.

We live the world we've built, drawing it ourselves to the point that we are plunged and wallowing in a system that awards success, son of hyper-productivity, and that demolishes everything else, causing damages that affect every aspect of our existence. Our economy times oblige us to work a lot (always connected), not to sleep much, to eat badly, not to work out enough, resulting in not only being more and more tired, but also getting sick more and more often.

Okay, we no longer die at 35 years old as our ancestors barely down from the trees, and actually – on a planetary level – we're progressively getting old, but from here to live well it would take quite a while/some time, isn't it?

The precariousness of the gig economy forces us to get up early, and to go to sleep late, causing constant sleep deprivation to 30% of the global population. Many of the products sold in supermarkets and restaurant chains are pseudo-food, crammed with refined/ processed sugar and harmful fats. The style of our everyday routine such as bad food, sloth habits, chronic stress and not enough sleep and laughter, causes 30% of us to suffer disorders of the digestive system (the irritable bowel syndrome, do you know?), that is also one of the main sources of a fast-growing disorder as depression, since more than 90% of the serotonin – feel-good hormone – is produced by bacteria of the bowel.[*]

We will talk about it again soon, for now let's stay on the main topic of capital, linked to time and work and so well-being.

If working too much
in addition to not functioning
it's bad for our health,
why do we do it then?

A possible answer might be: because we can't do without it.

Who will foot the bill if we don't deliver this or that by the deadline?

Or because "that's what we do", above all in a universe in which stakhanovism [**] is a synonym of productivity and productivity that of success.

If we don't work a thousand hours a day,
we are losers.

---

[*]   A pharmacist named Francesco Fratto told me and in 2022 he published ""Intestino senza pensieri" (Worry-free bowel), released by Sperling & Kupfer.

[**]   by a certain Aleksej Grigor'evič Stachanov, a russian miner who, in 1935, beat all the previous records in coal mining and who became the propaganda testimonial aiming to push workers productivity to the maximum.

Or because in a universe in which all is a synonym of productivity and productivity that of success.

If we don't work a thousand hours a day, **we are losers**

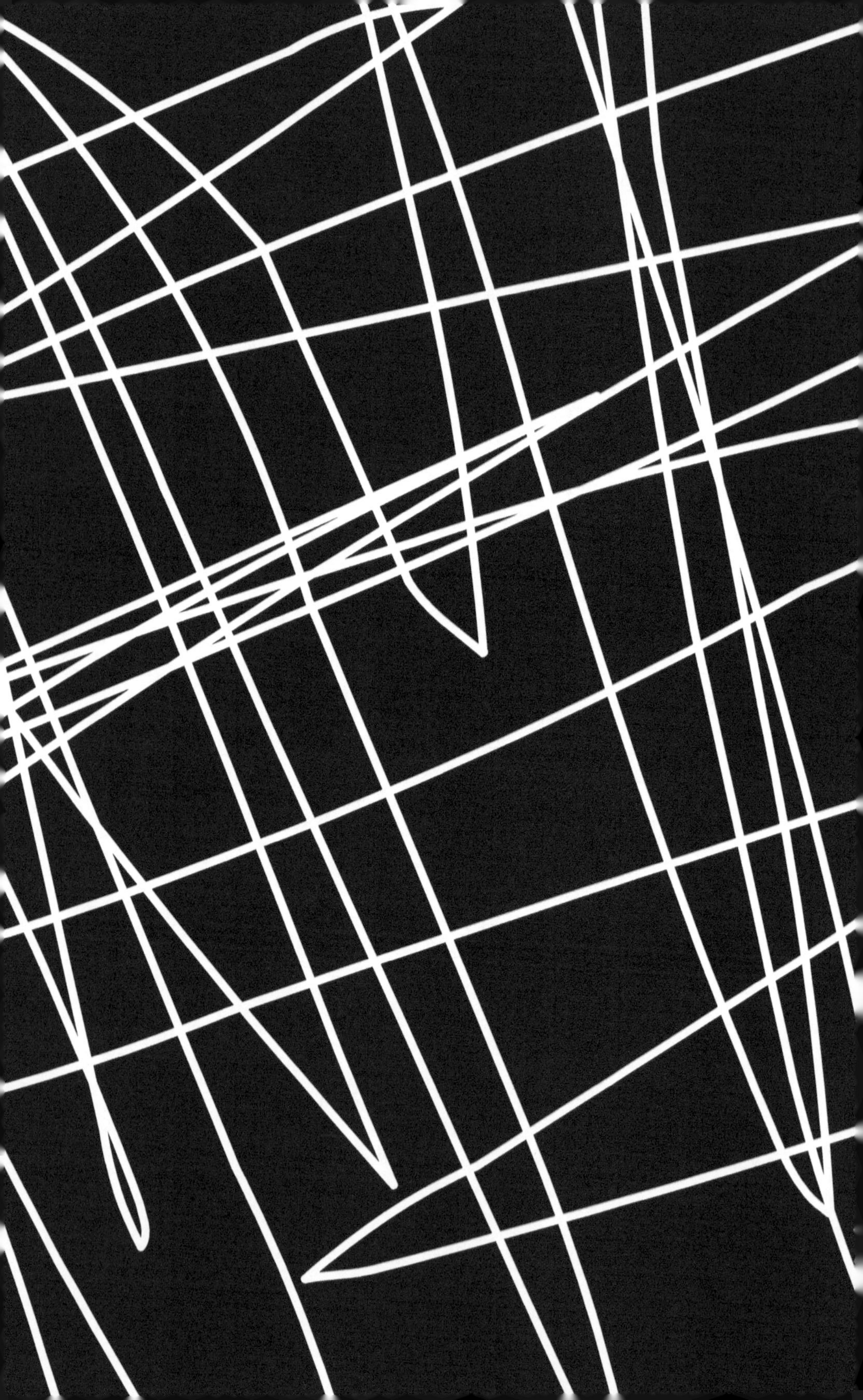

 # **OLD EMOTIONS, SAME FEAR**

Failures

We are failures if we are not rich, thin, pretty and happy enough. We are failures if we don't achieve our goals, if we don't manage to create enough engagement, if we don't get enough likes and shares.

And indeed, among the boomerang effects of the same gig economy we are fostering, we can find phenomena linked to the detachment between reality and expectations. Among them, unhappiness, sense of inadequacy / inferiority complex, anxiety and depression which are not at all born from social media.

Are they? And yet, it really seemed that Mario was about to tell us, again, that they are responsible for the evils of the world, including sadness, since they didn't keep their promises but they got us in trouble, etc…

Now, quoting a very old commercial with De Sica[*],
I think I didn't understand myself.

System

Social media are not Evil nor its cause, simply because, as I seem to have put between the lines, but maybe I'm wrong[**], social media are part of a system which is not an alien virus come from Andromeda to enslave us, but something that we wanted and we created, we humans, little people full of fears and high hopes, in perpetual fight between the former and the latter. Social media reflect something which comes from very very far, and that is older than Mathuselah and Tutankhamon: that is our brain, the same thing that invented the wheel and CHAT GPT, the same thing that built Taj Mahal, glasses, augmented reality visors, and *(another random thing, you decide)*.

---

[*]   Christian De Sica advertising ham in 1994.

[**]   I checked, I'm not.

Not a
thousand

Since we've stopped hunting pronghorn and wild berries, it seems around 10.000 B.C., in order not to die, we've always needed the same old things, not a thousand: food, water, shelter, sex and clan.

However, since none of these things are of much use if we get eaten by a sabre-toothed tiger, avoiding dangers quickly becomes the most relevant matter when it comes to survival. So much so that the brain developed learning exactly how to predict and to avoid threats.

Trial & Error

Through trials and errors, millennium after millennium, our slightly-more-than-a-kilo soggy and grey matter eventually became very good, reaching a pro-level which still today makes us constantly be alert so that we immediately understand whether something is good or bad, safe, dangerous, or potentially lethal or for the moment insignificant-and-then-we'll-see.

After learning to anticipate threats, or perhaps to do so in a better way, since wandering about in the wood alone put us at the risk of being spotted by the above-mentioned tiger or by wolves or by a myriad of other dangers that could eat us in a single bite, our brain immediately realized that in addition to food, water, shelter and sex, we needed company, we needed a group. And here is the clan from which derives the primordial need to fit in, otherwise the other possibility is exile, where we would find ourselves again among tigers and wolves.

To avoid being thrown out, we have learned to compare ourselves with other people of our group/clan and continuously ask ourselves whether we are settling in, whether we are liked and how much, or, if for some reason, other people are there to send us to exile.

Even though the challenge with the clan has exited forests, it still follows the same mechanisms it did before, leading us to a constant search for new ways to get better, to have more and thus to be appreciated even more.

How? With another myth, the one of productivity at all costs, the obsession and the foundation of time management of which Oliver Burkeman clearly writes: "we spend our days carrying out activities to get them out of our way. The result is that we live projected into the future (when we will finally be able to take care of what really matters) and that we fear that we won't measure up and don't have enough passion and energy to keep up with life today."[55]

The aim of doing everything in the right times and ways is to achieve success, and make a breakthrough, following myths different from each other, but almost all of them linked by the image of richer and more famous people, and therefore happier than we are.

"Many experiments have demonstrated that people manifest depression when they aren't able to live up to their ideals; instead, when they fail to meet standards established by other people, they feel anxious.[56]"

The problem is that today we have the same mechanisms of millions of years ago, but the size of social confrontation is quite different: if for our ancestors' clans it was a matter of pleasing a few people, for us the comparison is with a number of individuals potentially equal to the whole humanity. Or, at least, the part of humanity which has access to the Net.

Basically, even when we are in our bedrooms,

we are in front of a huge public.

Then, the picture gets more complicated with the machine that cranks out myths and rewards the people with the highest engagement, the richer, the more intelligent, the fitter, the happier than us, putting them in loop.

According to the 302 most important research about social media use and mental health, the psychological process of the former is linked to social confrontation, which is made even more intense, thick and intrusive by always being connected. From this derives the so-called FOMO, Fear of missing out, which is literally the fear of missing something happening on social media: "it is a form of social anxiety defined by an unpleasant sensation, or even devastating, that our fellows are doing something better than us and that they have more things or connections." Not to mention the annoying fact that over time our brain has also learned to imagine the best version of ourselves and it is exactly with that ideal that we are constantly obliged to compare ourselves.

And yet, it is not enough, because what makes it even more complicated, thus making us less happy than we could *(perhaps)* be, there are four myths about happiness which, from fairy tales to the cinema, do nothing but speak to us about happy endings, of happily ever after…

- Happiness is the natural condition of all human beings.
- If we are not happy, there's something wrong with us.
- In order to be happy, we should get rid of negative feelings.
- We should be able to control what we think and what we feel.

The first myth collapses under the weight of statistics *(**one adult out of ten attempts suicide, and one out of five suffers from depression**)*, and so it generates the second one, fostered by the conservative idea that every mental disorder or emotional discomfort is a symptom of weakness, and therefore a source of shame.

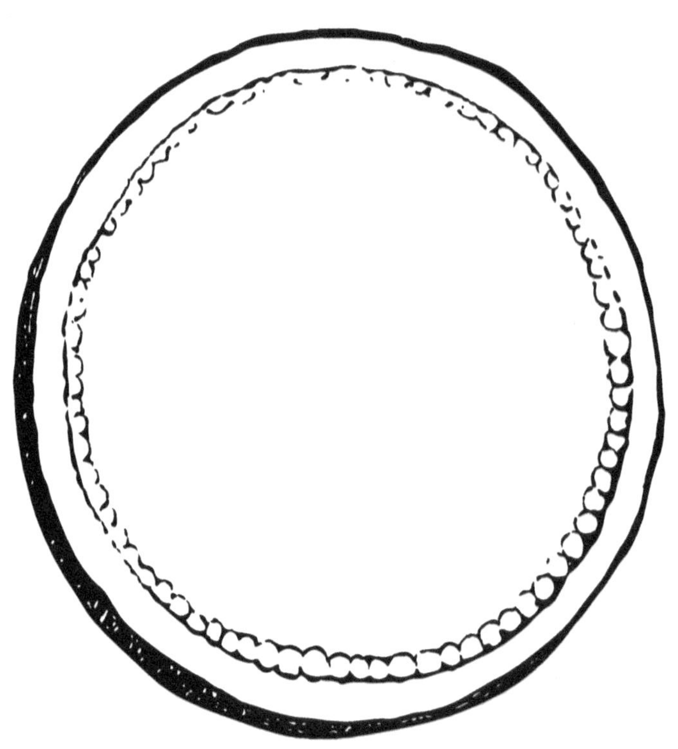

Draw your bouble identity

From this derives the third myth, preparatory to the next one[*] to live well, which means to be happy, we should only feel positive emotions.

And, finally, the fourth – as we said before, the consequence of number three – is the one on which the entire self-help industry is based, namely the illusion that it is always possible to control our thoughts, discarding the ugly ones in favour of unicorns and rainbows, regardless of whatever cataclysm happens to us.

Except that, our brain doesn't work like that, not at all, and so we feel inadequate, and gradually more sad, anxious, terribly depressed, especially because we don't live in the clans of our hairy ancestors anymore nor in the farmsteads of our great grandparents, but we live in the Net, and as I was saying, the continuous comparison with an infinite number of people happier than us *(and intelligent, and rich, and fit, etc…)* cannot but make us defeated to the point of escaping reality.

That's why we make it better with filters and/or we tell it with a baroque language. Or that's why many of us feel the need of having a double identity.

And also that's why we are desperately trying to create another one, like the ongoing experiments of – and in the metaverse, and in the meantime we end up isolating ourselves more and more, among other things convinced that we have many or more than many friends.

---

[*] Just like the exam of Maths II which you can do only after passing Maths I.

 # SINGULARITUDE

HERE IS WHERE WE TALK ABOUT TEENY-TINY HOUSES, SINGULARITUDE
AND SOLITUDE, HIKIKOMORI, AND OLD PHONES.

Has the world become small?
Our food certainly has: in about twenty years hypermarkets
and supermarkets went from family packs to couple packs to
single-dose packaging, designed and packed for singles.

Our houses have become smaller as well, because of
the terrible financial crisis in 2008, which has produced two
phenomena that came with happy narratives - tiny houses and
decluttering - both of them following the "less is more" trend,
an answer to the need to save money and avoid waste.

The sources[57] state that there were many properties under
40 sqm in 2018. For New York, Seattle, and San Francisco,
there was growing interest in living spaces of 25 to 37 square
metres. Similarly, as many as 25,000 micro-apartments had
recently been opened in Berlin, Frankfurt and Hamburg; while
in Italy, in Milan demand for homes up to 50 square metres
traded in 2017 was up 14% compared to the previous year. This
was followed by Turin and Naples, and Rome.

In 2020 during the Covid-lockdown many people had
to experiment the so-called smart working, someone for the
first time ever, in these very mini-houses, designed as dorms.
Multinational corporations and big corps reacted quickly,
having soon realised that not having physical offices, or
reducing them to the bare essentials, could - and is - a smart
way to reduce consumption, as well as costs.

Forced confinement has isolated us, making us
experience for ourselves and on our own skin that loneliness is
bad for our bodies *(for our bodies, our minds, for everything)* and
that good old Socrates was right, when he told Plato that man
is a social animal.

Even though we baked square metres of homemade pasta and
bread, and made videocalls and videoparties, not being able
to leave our tiny-houses showed us that meeting friends online
is not enough: in order to be well, especially in our head, we
need real interactions with real people.

However, at least in Italy, lockdown was less
devastating than we had feared, as it is shown in a study
published by Journal of Affective Disorders*, which reveals
that, firstly, psychological disorders have risen at the same
time as the pandemic, increasing the levels of anxiety and
depression, and then that they decreased 14 months after the
emergency, showing that, in the long run, they affected our
mental health less than it had been expected.

Confined in ever narrower spaces, we are lonelier than ever.

On one side of the monitor there's an entire planet within
a click's reach, while on the other our blood-and-flesh clan has
become smaller: smaller families, scattered around here and there,
more remote work and less in person.

By reducing our in-person interactions and increasing the
digital ones, the result we have is that we started to feel lonelier than
ever, to feel uneasiness. But instead of rebelling, our brain tried to use
its best asset, adaptation. What is happening while I'm writing this
is the mental and physical transition to a progressive self-isolating
condition, which we could call singularitude.

SINGULARITUDE
INCLINATION TO SINGULARITY AND SOLITUDE

Let's look at them one at a time.

---

*   In the study published by Journal of Affective Disorders, a team of
Italian researchers studied the progression of health problems in time linked to
the Covid-19 pandemic.

SINGULARITY

Singularity is the push towards technological progress which is so advanced that it goes beyond our ability to understand and foresee.

The word "singularity" appears for the first time in an essay published in 1993 by Vernon Vinge, where the author used this term to indicate the process in which creating machines which are increasingly smarter will lead to an ever-wider gap with human intelligence.

The Singularity is near *(written in 2006!)* by Ray Kurzweil**, is the book that contributed to making this word known to the general public.

"Not only is singularity inevitable, but the moment when AI will surpass human intelligence - we'll call it Turing point"- will come in a few decades."

Ray Kurzweil

When?
By 2025, says Kurzweil, "human beings will be creating machines which are smarter than them - a moment called "singularity". The intelligence of the machines will increase human intelligence in every area. Machines will be able to invent and improve themselves, further speeding up the pace of change".

**   Ray Kurzweil is the author of The Age of Intelligent Machines and The Age of Spiritual Machines and co-author, together with Terry Grossman, of Fantastic Voyage: Live Long Enough to Live Forever. He is an inventor who was awarded the National Medal of Technology in 1999.

AND SOLITUDE?

Solitude is a state which we are experiencing more and more often, so much so that it has become a lifestyle, as we can see with the phenomenon of *hikikomori*, from the Japanese word that indicates those people who decide to withdraw from social life for long periods of time, without any direct interaction with the outside world.

It seems that, in 2023, only in Japan, hikikomoris are over one and a half million.[58]

Between singularity and solitude, singularitude is a word that doesn't exist, but it has already become INCLINATION: a condition so widespread that even before understanding it, we normalized it.

Just as it has become normal to check our devices constantly, as soon as we wake up, during our coffee break, while driving and working, it is just as normal to do it while we are with other people, while eating, at dinner, with friends and loved ones, to the point that we have started talking about obsessions and smartphone addiction.

Between those who cry we are reaching the end of time, talking about obsessions and smartphone addiction, and those who minimise it, there are those who look for solutions by buying an old phone, like those designed for not-so-young-anymore people, and use it in their spare time.

In the meantime, a first wave of self-limiting tricks is catching on, like exposure time notifications. This tells us that even though our brains are trying to adapt, they probably have not managed to yet.

NAKED APES

Our brain is adapting and we're sure that sooner or later it will make it, even if we don't know how long the process will last; and even if in the meantime, we're facing a bunch of problems that we do not yet know how to deal with.

We're currently experiencing several discomforts that are affecting both our mind and body and they have consequences on the way we perceive the world and feel emotions. The fact that the body affects emotions is part of the so-called 'constructionism' or 'The Theory of constructed emotion': a line of thought that argues that our behaviours come from, in the immediate, biological processes that happen in our brain. And in our body.

Basically, to simplify, the emotions we feel aren't all the same, nor universal, nor even a consequence of our genes, but they are the result of a continuous process called interoception that takes place in each of us.

Interoception is the representation in our brain of all perceptions coming not only from internal organs and tissues, but also from the immune system and the endocrine one *(which regulates hormones)*. Essentially, interoception is the synthesis of the state of our body at that precise moment, which is the basic environment that determines the way we value and code what happens to us.

Once again simplifying, our body will induce us to perceive things that happen to us as more bothering if we keep doing the following things such as working too much, eating junk food, sleeping a little and badly, exposing ourselves to the artificial light of our tiny houses and of our devices for too many hours per day and we're moving fewer than we should. And therefore, this altered perception makes us feel sadder than we should.

183

When our body communicates to our brain that it's suffering, our brain applies a pejorative filter to our perception of the world. Otherwise, when our body is well the filter is optimistic.

Since our body hasn't gotten used yet to spend twelve/18 hours in front of a screen, nor to stay still for a very long time, nor to the artificial light and it doesn't want to know about modified food or overthink for entire nights, it's quite easy to understand why our poor body isn't well at all.

Our body is still ancient and resembles incredibly the one of our progenitors that evolved and abandoned their life on trees just as the ethologist Desmond Morris stated in his book, The Naked Ape - in Italian La Scimmia Nuda- at the end of 1960s. Since it's ancient, our body is at least trying to adapt, but while it does it, our body is struggling and therefore it suffers. Thanks to this, we can understand why psychological problems are increasing: if our body is ill and our filter is pejorative, then also our perceptions and emotions are negative.

That's why we cannot blame social media nor the GIG economy for all the evil in the world. By digging up everything we know about emotions and by smattering about how body, brain and emotions are connected and interdependent, we just get rid of an alibi.

I myself admit that in designing this book, while I was still just talking about it, I thought I'd self-flagellating: after all, I said to myself, it is also my fault if so, many people have come to feel uncomfortable with a system that I have helped to strengthen. Mine and those who like me, they were among the first to tell the world that anyone could open an online shop, find customers through social media, share valuable content, network, create engagement, etc.

But even though my expectations *(like those of other early adopters)* were very high, and the intentions excellent, they fuelled the mythological machine, helping to design the same world/perverse system economic and social system that we are complaining about today.

However, along with me, or rather well before me, on the podium of the of the guilty, were those few other individuals - at the head media and Big Tech - who made millions of dollars from the system to the millions of dollars, to the detriment of everyone else. Including myself.

After all, after the hunt for the antelope, the scapegoat hunt is the scapegoat is mankind's all-time favourite: we love to point the finger and blame someone else, so much so that we have built an entire narrative around the blame narrative, as well as the foundation of various religious currents and certain legal principles.

It is a pity that alibis and scapegoats hardly solve the problems. Instead, if we stop pointing the finger, or looking for a guilty elsewhere, we can start looking in the mirror and ask ourselves whether the system in which we live can be improved, and if so, how.

After all, if human intelligence has been able to think and write the artificial one, you want to see that it will be able to draw it to make our world a truly better world.

Or not?

"The wave of artificial workers that is coming will literally sweep the floor of the companies and will carry out our chores. We can take our dishwasher to the dump.[59]"

Jerry Kaplan

A New Era

With artificial intelligence, an era has begun, happy or terrible depending on the point of observation and observers, leading to a diametrically opposed perception.

A) As the latest, in the most recent sense, of human innovations, AIs are merely automations that we have built to make our lives easier, simplifying work and reducing costs.

B) Artificial intellects, despite being designed by human beings, will escape our control marking the advent of a hostile entity that will eventually enslave us, as in the worst of the Black Mirror episodes. For this entity, we also have a name: singleton.

Aliens

According to Geoffrey Hinton,[60] the new generation of large language models dimensions, in particular Chat Gpt, could be aliens:

"These things are totally different from us. Sometimes I think it's as if aliens had landed and people haven't realized because they speak very good English."

Geoffrey Hinton

Aliens, therefore, who could have landed among us without being recognised as such, since they speak excellent English...

187

Again, we find ourselves in an ambiguous situation, which our brain is forced to 'disambiguate', resorting to images that come from the past to decode possible future threats.

Hinton also believes that we may face several problems, including getting more and more whistles for flops and witnessing choices that are anything but choices that are anything but ethical.

1) Given the speed at which AI improve, and learn new functions, we may lose the ability to distinguish what is true and what is false, as has already happened to us with the image of the Pope dressed in a designer coat, and as could happen again, so much so that recognising a deepfake may not be easy, or even possible.

2) Since the next step of intelligent machines will be the ability to create their own sub-goals, i.e. intermediate steps necessary to complete a task, this capability could be applied to choices that go against our value system, not necessarily the same as theirs.

188

Hinton's concerns prompted him to leave Google, and not to 'speak ill of it', but to deal with it full-time, also because, as he himself said, after turning 75, he realised he was no longer as good as he used to be.

"I'm getting too old to do technical work that requires remembering lots of details. I'm still okay, but I'm not nearly as good as I was, and that's annoying." [61]

And so, Hinton has joined the herd of exiles, came out from Big Tech, among whom there are many who say they are scared.

Faced with professions and entire markets that are already at risk, ready to be wiped out, perhaps waiting for those still in the making, optimists and pessimists are both aware of the distortions and the inevitable damages.

What makes the difference in their respective perspectives and prophecies, perhaps, is something to do with confidence, which in the former abounds and in the latter is lacking.

For example, the questions that Nick Bostrom, Professor at Oxford University and founder of the Future of Humanity Institute, start from the fact that artificial intelligence has already surpassed our own in many areas, and above all that is based on the process of continuous self-improvement, could lead to an 'intelligence explosion' that would then result in 'one or more forms of superintelligence":

- superintelligence of speed;
- collective superintelligence;
- quality superintelligence.

The 'fast super-intelligence' could replicate human intelligence human intelligence but work much faster.

The 'collective super-intelligence' would be a group of subsystems written by individuals enhanced by engineering-enhanced individuals genetics, capable of independently solving discrete problems within a large project (such as the development of the Space Shuttle).

The third, defined as 'quality superintelligence', refers to an artificial intelligence of such high quality as to be superior to human intelligence as is ours than that of dolphins or chimpanzees.

Back to singularity

A fundamental point of Bostrom's studies touches on the concept of orthogonality, which he explains by telling us that the character of AI and, by extension, of superintelligence, is not expressly human.

"Fantasies about humanised AI are misleading. Although perhaps counterintuitive, the orthogonality thesis holds that intelligence levels are not related to ultimate goals. Higher intelligence does not necessarily imply common or shared goals among different AIs."

In framing the promise of a safer, rich, and intelligent world, Bostrom's vision is as optimistic as it is critical, putting on the page (indeed, in 520 pages) the doubt of a humanity that may not be ready.

To do what?

To begin with, we may not be able to upload our values with the certainty that they will be received and interpreted to our advantage. And then there is no guarantee that AI will remain 'friendly', i.e. continues to work for us, instead of turning into a Singleton.

If in fact AI, or a super-intelligent agent AI combined, gained a 'decisive strategic advantage' as an entity in its own itself, we might no longer be able to control it.

"In front of us humans,
we are like little children playing with a bomb."
Children, who by the way, as AI grows and improve, may even get worse.

> Why strive to write better, and be more understandable, and/or appeal more to our readers if Ais can do it for us, and faster, even by intercepting the specific preferences of different user groups.

> Why learn maths when we can have our homework done from Chat GPT?

Such reasoning is part of the framework that led to the blocking of Chat GPT, as happened in January 2023 for American schools, and in April of the same year for entire nations, such as Italy.[62]

Given that mundane tasks such as answering emails, or doing research have already become useless, in addition to the human intelligence that is in danger of waning as synthetic intelligence grows, another issue of epochal significance concerns work. Again, back in 2016, Bostrom wrote about this in his People are not needed, explaining how AI is confusing the labour market in two ways.

"THE FIRST IS THAT AUTOMATION WILL REPLACE WORKERS, ELIMINATING THEIR JOBS. THE SECOND HAS TO DO WITH THE SPEED WITH WHICH IT IS ALREADY DOING SO."

ive super-intelligence' would be a group of
written by individuals enhanced by engineering-
individuals genetics, capable of independently
ete problems within a large project (such as the
the Space Shuttle).
third, defined as 'quality super-intelligence',
artificial intelligence of such high quality as to be
man intelligence as is ours than that of dolphins
ees.

Singularity

damental point of Bostrom's studies touches on
orthogonality, which he explains by telling us
acter of AI and, by extension, of superintelligence,
sly human.

bout humanised AI are misleading. Although
unterintuitive, the orthogonality thesis holds that
levels are not related to ultimate goals. Higher
does not necessarily imply common or shared
different AIs."

ming the promise of a safer, rich, and intelligent
m's vision is as optimistic as it is critical, putting
(indeed, in 520 pages) the doubt of a humanity
be ready.

gin with, we may not be able to upload our values
tainty that they will be received and interpreted
tage, and then there is no guarantee that it will
dly, i.e. continue to work for us, instead of turning
ton.

Whereas in the 19th century agriculture employed 80% of the workers in the United States, falling to 40% in 1900 and 1.5 % by the end of the century, the changes we are witnessing are occurring not over the course of one or two centuries, but from one decade to the next, at a speed that governments cannot understand, and therefore cannot keep up.

Entire categories of workers, at the first wave of CHAT GPT and its counterparts, began to falter. Among them, at the forefront, freelancers, copywriters, graphic designers editors, and programmers who, during a couple of months, have witnessed the release of the beta versions, have tried them out and have discussed them, sharing - obviously – their opinions on social media.

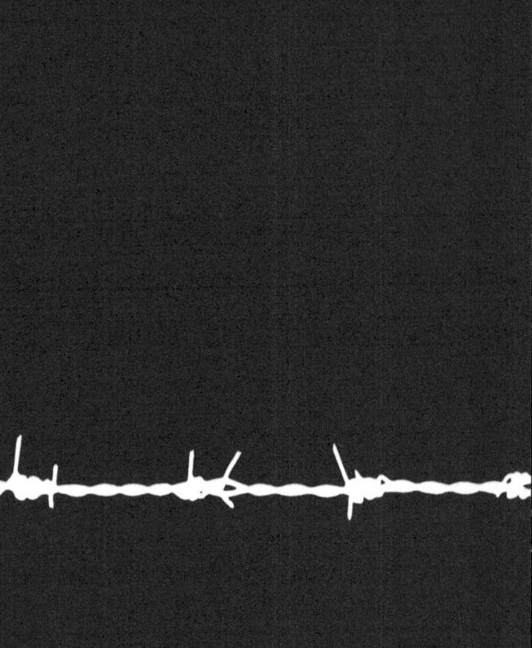

FRONTIER

Between those who say that AI products are better, those who are convinced they are much worse, and those who wanna play Switzerland and not take sides, claiming that they are not comparable, let's try to bring a tiny bit of clarity to the matter.

› AI is **better** when it reduces the time and cost of the product by automating some tedious and boring, as well as not really useful steps, and it is better not only for the buyer but also for those who are working on the product in question.

› Synthetic intelligences are **worse**, much worse when they show us that they are abundantly capable of selling us fireflies for lanterns and doing so at the speed of light, such as - to cite one example - the matter of the "Papa Balenciaga" fake news. The ease with which AIs create fake images that seem more real than reality leads us to fear that identity theft may become - or already is - not the prerogative of a few geeks on the deep web, and wizards of photo-editing programs, but open, exactly as are much of AI themselves.

On the other hand, AI is a new tool, just as was, back in the day, the calculator that reduced the time of calculations and made everyone who did nothing but calculations useless. Just like the press, or the plow. Only, in the case of the plow *(and of other machines that automated agriculture)*, the economic and social mutation took place over centuries, while the current one changes our market within one or two seasons.

It's not just tedious activities that are at risk but also those in which our creativity and intuition do or should make a difference, like everything pertaining to the work of journalists, writers, screenwriters, lawyers, and doctors, all people who have invested a good part of their lives to learn professions that are faltering today. So, it's not just individual professions that are faltering, but entire markets, such as the automotive, for example.

Okay, we are not ready for the so-called "driverless cars", but neither were we at the beginning of the 20th century, when the first automobiles appeared, so much so that for a while we called them "driverless carriages".[63]

But even if we are not ready, they will come, tearing to shreds not only their own market but also the satellite activities. The power and speed of AIs are such that it is only a short time before we will no longer need to buy a book hoping that we will like it, except sometimes to be so disappointed that we will ditch it by the third page: we will be able to have it written directly by a synthetic intellect that's in tune with our taste, with the plot we like best and even in the style we prefer.

In just a few, very few months, artificial intelligences have swooped down on us better, much better, than we would have ever expected. They have defeated the competition by benching the metaverses, even before metaverses aspired to become public knowledge.

Caught up in a sincere enthusiasm *(or a sincere breakdown psychic)*, we needed time to process the event. In the meantime, AIs have invaded every possible and imaginable sector of the Earth System: an entire class of brainiacs captained by Go Charlie, Dall-e, Namelix, Notion, Synthesia, Runway, Thispersondoesnotexist and blah blah blah.

The latest AIs?

Mixo, a website creation tool; Canva, which creates stunning images with the click of a button; Midjourney v5 which can design high-quality graphics with 3D models, animations and other visual effects; and then all those focused on sales

196

such as ZonGuru and Jungle Scout used by Amazon, or Perci for text and Quartile to perform sectorial analysis.

AIs, they are everywhere.

Even H&M Group *(yes, **that's right, the fast fashion one**)* has launched one: it is Creator Studio[64], a platform to produce merchandising, which uses generative artificial intelligence to make anyone capable of creating and printing professional-looking designs on demand, with no artistic ability required.

As for price, the best tools, needless to say, require a fee. Of course, there are trial versions, the basic ones, also called pie without fruit or sugar.

But they say little to nothing about the real capabilities of these AIs, and subscriptions basically become necessary to make proper use of them.

The first, and most famous, to confirm all of this is Chat Gpt, which, for twenty dollars a month, stops, for instance, responding to you with a two-year, almost three-year delay.

And it's already been a year since that November 2022 when Chat Gpt entered our lives, kicking off the long list of:

"and now we're screwed."

Because, shall we say, ethical and moral controversies have already filled endless parcels of legal paperwork. Starting with the concerns of teachers and professors who we have seen block and censor the system to a great extent, all the way to authors.

Some time ago, novelist Douglas Preston challenged ChatGpt by asking her *(/him)* to write an original poem based on a character from one of his books.

The result?

Wicked.

"What really surprised me was how much she knew about this character; much more than she could have gathered from the Internet", said Preston[65], adding that the feeling was not much different from coming home and finding out that someone had stolen all your stuff.

This is the reason why Preston started, shortly after, a "class action" against the developers of Chat Gpt for copyright infringement. Supported in the lawsuit by a number of other big-name authors, including John Grisham, Jonathan Franzen, Jodi Picoult and George R.R. Martin *(father of Game of Thrones)* who was very concerned that his fans would use the very bot to generate in advance the latest highly anticipated book of the series.

And of little use were the calm and soothing responses from Chat Gpt *(i.e., the humans behind Chat Gpt)* because as reported by Ed Nawotka, editor of Publishers Weekly, "All authors realize to what extent their data, their information, their creativity, have been absorbed, and there is, in the industry, a certain degree of petty panic."

All while OpenAI simply refuses to answer the question about whether the plaintiffs' books are part of the Chat Gpt training data or accessible via file-sharing sites such as LibGen.[66]

Thousands of writers* then decided to sign a letter in which they asked OpenAI, but also Meta, to stop using their work without permission or compensation. This is just the latest counter-offensive in chronological order that the literary world has launched against AI.

---

*　　Among them are Nora Roberts, Viet Thanh Nguyen, Michael Chabon and Margaret Atwood.

But protecting writers from the negative impact of these technologies is no piece of cake because artificial intelligences that are capable of generating text such as Gpt-4 and Bard, effectively scrape the Web in search of authored content without permission or compensation to produce new content in response to user requests.

It's what they were programmed to do.

And that only gives the final blow to a sector, the authorship sector to be exact, that is already in the midst of a full-fledged, crisis as seen by the -42% drop in revenue from 2009 to 2019.

The concern is great and as reported by Alexander Chee, the bestselling author of novels such as "Edinburgh" and "The Queen of the Night": *There is no urgent need for AI to write a novel"* as if to say that writers who can do it, and well, there are plenty of, but, he adds, *"the only people who might need it are the only ones who object to paying writers what they are worth."*

Touchè.

In response in the United States, India, and Japan, Google has begun releasing a new form of generative AI-powered search. The product is called Search Generative Experience or SGE.

SGE uses artificial intelligence to create summaries for some search questions. A kind of insight is placed at the top of the page as if to say: here you go, here you can find more on the topic, that has been well screened and selected specifically for you.

199

This literally drove publishers, who have been loudly shouting their concern, crazy, as they were sure of the fact that they would once again be robbed of content without any profit; even though, all things considered, they can do little against Google.

Their "unusual reaction"[67] to the search giant leads them to be dependent on online advertising which now threatens their copyrights.

However, Google, bless their good heart, has stated that "if publishers want to prevent their content from being used by Google's AI to create such summaries, they should use the same tool that would prevent them from appearing in Google's search results." This, simply put, would make it impossible for people using the search option to find publishers who choose not to be involved in SGE.

A total scam, basically.

For what concerns the "Belpaese," at the end of October 2023, the Italian Government has chosen to entrust the leadership of the new commission on artificial intelligence in publishing - already renamed the algorithms commission - to 85-year-old Giuliano Amato.[68]

And while it is now well established that artificial intelligences feed on what humans produce, like Alien projected outside our brains, there is no way to put an end to their unstoppable growth *(and I'm being dramatic, that is, unless we end our own existence).*

Nevertheless, we can poison them.

And I think it was precisely this thought process that gave life to Nightshade, the "poison" with which we aim to modify the pixels of the creations of human authors and artists, before they are introduced to the web, to hide them from the phagocyting bots. [69]

Modifications that are imperceptible to the human eye but capable of completely sending AIs into a tailspin, such as:

I published a cow for you to take as a sheep.

Whether these will be the new frontiers of human-machine coexistence is too early to tell. Certainly, since the first AI Act, dating May 2023, in which the European Community drew up a set of levels of risk concerning violations of artificial intelligences against the fundamental rights of the individual, to the use of poisons with which to kill the monster, a lot of water has passed under the bridge.

But it is good to remind my past and present self that progress cannot be stopped and that there is still a difference, in 2023, between what an AI produces and the creation of a hand, but what we don't like to think about is that the difference is already thin and will continue to get thinner, which will open the doors to reconfiguring the market between customers who are hostile to AI, based on principle or momentary distrust, and enthusiastic early-adopters.

For a while - and don't ask me to make predictions - creatives will still have customers to sell their creative products to, and publishers will still be looking for human writers, but sooner or later we will have to get used tointegration, as surgeons operating side by side with robots have already learned to do.

The New Frontier

AIs are the new frontier: not *(only)* of jobs, income, and certainly not of technology, but of society, and they are *(almost)* ready to become the new social media.

As a new frontier, since most of us agree on this, it is appropriate to treat them as such, perhaps taking a cue from history, so as not to repeat tomorrow, or rather today, the mistakes of yesterday.

And if there is one thing we can learn from history, it is that the frontiers change, boundaries shift, some faster than others, as has already happened to Open AI, with the sacking on the spot of its CEO, Sam Altman, dismissed by his own board on Nov. 17, 2023, and followed by several titans, including co-founder Greg Brockman, all within a week after he had attended an event with Microsoft, which had recently invested a whopping $13 billion in Open AI specifically.

During a special episode of "The Caffettino"[70], which aired on Sunday, November 19, '23, I talked about it with Giuseppe Mayer - Managing Partner @ Antifragile, Investor & Digital Advisor, Author & Keynote Speaker - who in an article[71] on LinkedIn said that the possible "end" of Open AI might not be bad news, but "the catalyst that stimulates greater competition."

In the chaotic end of 2023, we have therefore witnessed the 'drama' of Sam Altman leaving, then returning, then flirting with Microsoft, and then reconsidering again in OpenAI. A true corporate soap opera that some reduce to mere whims of the board of directors. I, on the other hand, prefer putting on my detective hat and digging deeper into this intricate corporate soap opera.

And then there's Microsoft, which, with a modest investment of one billion dollars in OpenAI, has practically got its hands on the board of directors, making the word 'Open' magically vanish from OpenAI.

Open-source principles?

Ah, those old romantic ideals have been kindly escorted off the premises. We seem to have once again decided to entrust the future of technology to the favorite game of capitalism: the mark.

```cpp
#INCLUDE <IOSTREAM>

    INT MAIN ( )

(

STD::COUT << "HELLO WORLD,

        I AM THE ALGORITHM!" << STD::ENDL;

RETURN 0;

)
```

THE MASTER OF ALGORITHM IS IGNORING US

HERE IS WHERE WE FACE THE ALGORITHM

"The so-called social media are created for consumption and advertising, but not for people. Now that they are collapsing, how can we create a real alternative?"

Wired was already wondering about it in November 2022, when it wrote about the fact that our social media homepages have no longer been populated by our friends/our communities for years. Instead, they are populated by contents chosen for us by "inscrutable algorithms, which, in turn, can be bypassed by advertisers who pay to push or promote their posts".

These algorithms are all around us, and they are all around us since the revolution that started with the automated learning, which is the basis of the machine-learning, as Pedro Domingos explained in the now distant 2015 in his 'The Master Algorithm - How the Quest for the Ultimate Learning Machine Will Remake Our World'.

"Machine learning is a novelty under the spotlight: a technology that creates itself."

You interact with the machine learning every day.

It is the machine learning that is in action when Netflix suggests you a movie or a search engine completes your query,. It is a revolution. Throughout history, if you wanted a machine to do something, you had to create it to do exactly that. For computers, you used to write a detailed algorithm explaining how it should do what you wanted it to do.

The algorithm that we have fueled and trained by ourselves chooses at our place: it proposes uninteresting and annoying contents to the point of forcing us to look for ruses to avoid it.

An example in the entertainment field concerns streaming platforms where we are forced to create new profiles, jump from one platform to the other *(paying with new subscriptions and/or data)* or look for possible unlock codes *(on social media, btw)* to avoid being bombarded, as usual, by the four identical series.

As we have seen several times throughout this book, since the goal sticks to the customer, which is the advertiser, the platforms where we still move are anything but 'social'. And, in fact, they are media.

After years of scandals, Facebook has imploded. Instagram has become unbearable. Twitter, which was already facing a ,ass exodus after Elon Musk's takeover, has been described as a "social ghost", since 10 per cent of its users represent 90 per cent of traffic and its "most frequent users" don't post even once a day.

While evolving fast into media, the old social media have disappointed expectations, not actually including anymore the communities on which they are founded and on which - let us not forget - they stand. The result is that the same algorithm, which is supposed to learn and improve constantly to supply even more suitable contents, ignores us. That is why then, many have already said *#ciaone.*

Cut the page in half.

A LONG LONG TIME AGO…

HERE'S WHERE WE TELL A FAIRY TALE

Stargate

A long, long time ago, there was the early adopter, a young hero full of hope, exploring for a new, better world, in front of which, from his brand-new Stargate, he saw an entire universe with the potential of being more free, democratic, rich and happy.

What the young hero didn't know, was that he was in front of a cave inhabited by the trainers of a dragon, a beast who could change form and who would soon enchant and imprison him to eat him and his contents, his preferences, his every single movement, to then make him the same poor slave from his myths, a Narcissus capable of only loving himself and not others, and dies of starvation for this very reason, and a Myda so obsessed with gold he can no longer eat.

Dominated

Now dominated by the dragon, one step near the singularity, pressed by the singularitude, trapped in the hive and a subject of the consumer-centred economy, the poor little human being even found himself, at the beginning of the first twenty years of the third millennium, a prisoner of a global pandemic.

From the prison called lockdown, the hero started to look outside, asking himself if life was worth living in such a bad way. And that's when the young human being understood he only had one life, not a thousand, just like the rosiest of metaverses, and so he forged a shield he called YOLO and with that, he started to dream of woods and forests, of trucks and mini-van, and, in the meantime, for the first time in a long long time, of setting foot outside the dragon's cave, starting what in the future centuries would be called the great exodus.

209

YOLO

YOLO is just an acronym, the umpteenth one, made from the letters composing the sentence YOU ONLY LIVE ONCE, but it's also the sign that in the air, or rather, in the ether, a new virus is starting to circulate: the need to free ourselves from the chains of the dragon, to get out the hive, say a big fat goodbye *(ciaone)* to the GIG economy and, maybe, finally transform the social/the future in the place and future we deserve to have.

While on standby for this to succeed, the exodus has started, leaving in the BIG-TECH-cave only a few categories of survivors.

Among these, aside from myself, are Fabrizio, Lara, Gloria and Walter, that is the people to whom I'm writing these lines. Just like me and every member of the community addicted to social, they will be the last ones to flee *(that is, if it's necessary, which is not to be taken for granted, as we will see in five minutes).*

Outside the world of social, in the meantime, the world is ageing, just as stated by the World Social Report 2023, which estimates that by 2050 the over 65 will be more than doubled.

Sure, the survival of the species very much likes ageing, thanks a lot, since we live longer, but insurance companies, pensions and the economy like it way less, even if they like the wisdom of the ty, but they still need young people in order to work and stay on their feet.

Let's not talk about innovations and revolutions …

Then, as the planet turns white, gets a paunch and experiences backache, so does the social and, obviously, so does the population that still frequents them and their even more *#cringe,* embarrassing contents which push even more youngsters to take to one's heels.

And actually, they were the first ones to flee.

Some simply deactivated their accounts, others, by making it a movement, like the YOLO, didn't deactivate their accounts, but still abandoned the logic of the hive in favour of a more minimalist, simple and direct philosophy:

- ☑ ~~Less obsession for s-~~ ~~uccess and richness~~
- ☑ ~~Fewer things,~~
- ☑ ~~Less hassle,~~
- ☐ More life.

Just as demonstrated by the flight of the Big Tech of many ex-early adopters, who were also trainers of the Dragon, like the already quoted Jaron Lanier, who was only a pioneer.

Or like the teenagers in Brooklyn with their #LUDDITECLUB.

#LudditeClub

Some teenagers from #Brooklyn understood the super powerful toll the #socialnetwork had on their mental health and decided to abandon them. So they took out their flip phones, just for necessary calls, and they meet every Sunday at the Central Library.
What for? To read, talk, play the guitar...

just as we did some years ago.

In the meantime, the same media are looking for alternatives, just as Meta, which, in April 2023, declared they were "exploring a standalone decentralised social network for sharing text updates."[72].

What does it mean? A new Twitter, but created on a decentralised network based on the Mastodon model to give more voice to the micro-communities.

AGAINST YOUTH

HERE'S WHERE IT'S BETTER TO LEAVE IT TO THE YOUTH

"This youth is rotten to the core. The youth are malignant and slothful. They will never be like the youth of old times. Today's youth will not be able to preserve our culture"

It's been since the time of Babylon the Great that those who are no longer young have been bad-mouthing the youth, based on the inscription quoted above which dates as far back as 3000 B.C., or in the following two sentences, attributed to Hesiod and Socrates respectively.

"There is no hope for the future of our country if today's youth seizes power tomorrow. This youth is unbearable, shameless, terrible."

"Our youth loves luxury, is rude, mocks authority, and has no respect for elders. Today's children are tyrants, they do not stand up when an old man enters the room, they talk back to their parents. In a word. They are bad."

Over the centuries, we have always liked to point the finger at young people to blame them for all or almost all of our world's woes, but in recent years, we have widened our target, so much that today, among the ones responsible for the collective unease, in addition to young people with no prospects in countries where welfare is in the hands of the families and not of the state, for whom, perhaps, going abroad is no longer enough, we also include 'anaesthetised, demotivated, depressed' 30-year-olds and over-40s who are unable to make ends meet.

The new 'lost generation' is between 15 and 50 years old, or 12 - 60, because in addition to growing up earlier, as the 40 have become the new 30 and then the 50 the new 40, then we grow old later *(and better)*.*

Excluding age, our lost generation seems to lack the strength to change things, because of, according to Zuboff**, the perverse logic into which we have got ourselves. Meanwhile, Mark Fisher talks to us about a capitalist realism that we believe it sucks, but cannot change, because we are past the point of wanting to, all while Jerry Kaplan and Nick Bostrom and Pedro Domingos try to make us realise, at least a little, that the singularity is near, and we must open our eyes and do something about it. Meanwhile, the drums of trolls tell us that the networks never existed, and the media are collapsing, hand in hand with the great exodus.

---

*   See the trend #agegracefully of the first years of the Twenties
**   And not just her, obviously

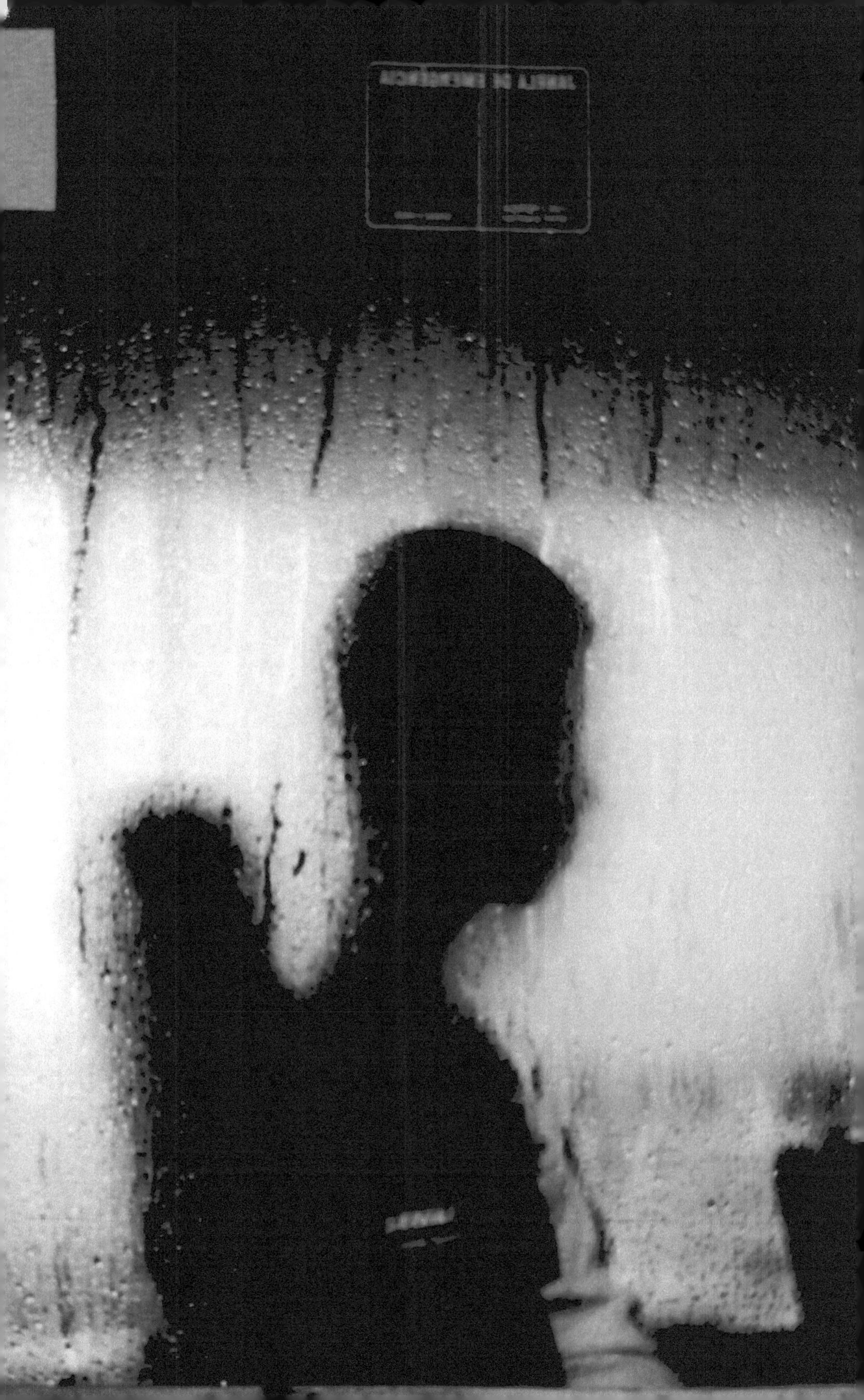

SOCIALSOF THETUTURE THEFUTURE OFSOCIALS

REVOLUTION

We've spoken a lot about the fact that we need to take action, and like I hope to have at least in part shown, there are many rumours going around, way more influential than my own voice.

So, a revolution is needed. Or, at least, that's what people say...

"On social networks people are insistently asking for a revolution as the only possible radical change coming from an anger, from a frustration and from a dissatisfaction push."

Lots of people have been saying it, and for a while now, because we've finally noticed it. But, as always, it's easier said than done and for people like us – namely those like Fabrizio, Lara, Gloria, Walter and Mario – it's also a question of putting food on the table. According to Professor Galimberti, a super reliable source, the trouble is that at the moment we are missing essential things for a revolution. And, since these things are (*at least*) four, the matter gets tricky.

1he first problem is that each revolution breaks out when the interests of two opposite sides clash, for example lords and servants or bosses and subordinates. But today they are on the same side and their opponent is the market, a rival without face and will.

That's to say, nobody.

And, as Galimberti explains, even if Homer said that Nobody is always someone's name, the problem is that our Nobody has no face, and so we don't know who to blame.

"West is a word meaning sunset,
        it has its fate written in its name."

Galimberti

2 The second problem is that, so as to keep our current welfare state, the West – 18% of the world population – needs 80% of the Earth resources.

"If Indian or Chinese people eat one more bowl of rice, just like that we are forced to reduce our consumptions and way of life. Nobles had big castles, but after the emergence of the middle class they couldn't live there anymore because it was too expensive. Likewise, our children won't be able to keep our houses, which have until now represented our wealth."[73]

3 The third problem is that revolutions have always been started by young people. You just try to face a tank with your grandma's walker and see what happens... It's young people that protest, make themselves heard, try to find alternative solutions and lead all of the revolutions, not just because they are naturally more agile than mommy and daddy and the grandparents, but also because they are definitely smarter.

- ☑ They learn quicker
- ☑ They know more things
- ☑ They react faster
- ☑ And they stand less in their own way (*surely less than us, among others*)

Basically, young people and not so young people have as much in common as artificial intelligence and human intelligence: six to zero, it's not even a competition ladies and gentlemen, end of story.

4 The fourth problem is that young people aren't up to it, or not enough but – as the history of revolutions teaches us – the desire shows up when hunger comes, which we, at least in the West, don't feel for now. Even an old Arabic saying says it: "Hard times create strong people, strong people create good times. Good times create weak people and weak people create hard times.*"

Since the world as we know it will disappear, it's time to face a forced but conscious degrowth, driven by values which start with retiring the GIG economy. Moving the customer from the center, for example, completely putting them aside, means replacing them with what is now ignored: the territory, the planet, other people. These are the elements that we need to start considering as non-fungible resources and to give them the white-glove treatment *(and no, not the metaverse one)*.

All of this, always according to the teach., will not be possible unless made compulsory, so something forced, that imposes we consume less, eat less, spend less. In a nutshell go back to when we were completely broke. And yet it moves, as Galilei seems to have said in front of the inquisition court. Since the new generations are already smarter than the immediately previous ones *(so much so that for super young people a luxury car isn't a status symbol anymore, nor a value)*, we should rely on them to create our new world, social media included..

So?

#FIDATY (#HAVE-TRUST) Mario.
Ask them, the young people, how to redesign the world, maybe starting exactly from social networks

---

*   I took the freedom to replace the word "men" with "people".

MICRO

PAY
THE LAND

PAY THE
CREATORS

IDENTITY

I WISH A SUPER SOCIAL
MICRO SOCIAL

» Hi, I'm Mario and I'm an early adopter.
» Hi Mario, welcome, do you want to share?

No, I don't want to, or better, I would like to tell you that social network I want today are the exact opposite of how I wanted them 20 years ago, but the truth is that I'm too old to be part of revolution we are hoping for, and so nothing, I leave the floor and pass, with pleasure, the microphone to the young people.

What follows, I must warn you, it is neither a receipt nor the ingredients for a magic formula that is capable by itself to rebuild an entire world with people, including us, that have several nuisances to solve every day.
So, let's say that it is sort of vision board on which I will try to stick post-its.

Another warning: the post-its I'm about to stick are not all my own doing, but they arrived at my mill thanks to the people that follow my work. Among them, Lara, Fabrizio, Gloria e Walter but also others for a scarce amount of some twenty, or so, of young people, who over time either have answered my questions or have given their ideas for free.

Too few to be meaningful
in terms of research?

If it was a quantitative research based on statistics, okay, but in this case, it's about a qualitative research: few people, but with the same interests.

Since one of the problems that plague us is precisely knowing the users' identity, i.e. knowing with whom we are interacting with and at the meantime letting the others know our real identity, a possible idea would be using the identity card, in order to authenticate ourselves uniquely, and thus get rid at a moment's notice with a lot of trolls and mean people, who hide behind anonymity to spread hate and other shit.

In this way, if we want to express our opinion, we become responsible for what we say. This, of course, will maybe limit our freedom of opinion, but this forcing/constriction will oblige us to think it through before to talk nonsense. In its turn, "thinking it through" means reducing our speed of interaction, extending everyone's time, and thus beginning to move away from the just-in-time logics, that is the principal source of bad capitalism, environment cataclysms, stress and other ills.

The key concept of this post-it is responsibility: the moment to take responsibility every day for our choices has come and, for example, by stopping looking for somebody else, even for the Big Other, to blame and beginning to reduce consumptions, standard and fluff.

» Less FOAM, less running against time,

less obsession for money and success.

224

Paying the territory, namely the platform: paying for what we really want to see, could give us what we really want to see.

Saying it in this way, it seems a shot of the old general La Palice, from whom we took the expression "lapalissian" but thinking it through: on the one side, as human being we have always had a problem with free things, simply because the more we pay a thing, the more we perceive its values; on the other side, if it's true that it is free, we are NOT the product, but, as we've said, we are still the raw material, therefore the part of the process that make the system bill.

If the platforms are paid, it means that in order to enter we have to pay and this could allow us to take two kill two birds with one stone:

- If we pay the platform, it must not be filled with advertisements.
- f we pay, like hell the platform shares our data and the call centres harasses us two thousand times a day.
- If we don't like what we see, we can go away and stop paying.

The key point here is that professor Galimberti may be right in telling us that we cannot make a revolution, because we don't have an enemy to fight against, being this enemy nameless and faceless, but at least, if we removed the advertisement purpose from media, we would take away those very weapons that we find ourselves against today.

225

To pay contents, or rather the contents creators. As we have previous seen, to pay for what we really want to see could give us what we really want to see.

> The payer becomes the customer for whom the creator produces content.

There are already specific territories where the content creators receive contributions from their communities, for example Patreon, and they actually work.

#MICROCOMMUNITIES

From "all for all", to "little (*but good*) and only for someone".

The world GAME – global opened marvelous epic - prophesied by social networks, turned out to be the grotesque, suffocating, threatening, egocentric world of social media that have ignored their community *(namely us, their raw material and their real mean of spreading)* and it's led us to flee.
Or at least to dream to do it.

Social networks turn out to be in their entirety a fusion soup of stupid or polarized contents, appropriate for everyone and seasoned with myths and memes that the algorithm proposes us, on the basis of what attract us more and which, although it stupefies us, we rarely really like.

The logic of all for all is a chimera because "for all" means "for nobody", as a long time ago I have been told by a person who lives of writing, i.e. pays his bills and feeds his herd by doing nothing else but writing *(and reading)*.

226

In order to get out from this chimera of "all for all", we could begin to imagine social media made of and for the micro-community of people who – for a certain life period – are interested to a certain topic, only to later change topics and communities.

This change could solve then another issue, that is the monothematic one: if we stay all the time in the same community, we only learn from that and we end up modelling ourselves on that community until, after a while, we have nothing more to learn *(a bit like the logic of isolated villages and the same islands)*; if, on the other hand, we frequent a community for certain period, and later we begin to travel, exploring others, then we have the possibility to extend our horizons and thus to learn new things and receive different incentives.

It's a little bit the logic of Telegram, if you want.

It's a pity that also Telegram has become a playground for dealing in things that are anything but well-meaning, such as the affair of communities of would-be phishers exchanging tricks.

Other post-its, some random and some not.*

---

*   They are stuck to the blackboard without any specific order.

227

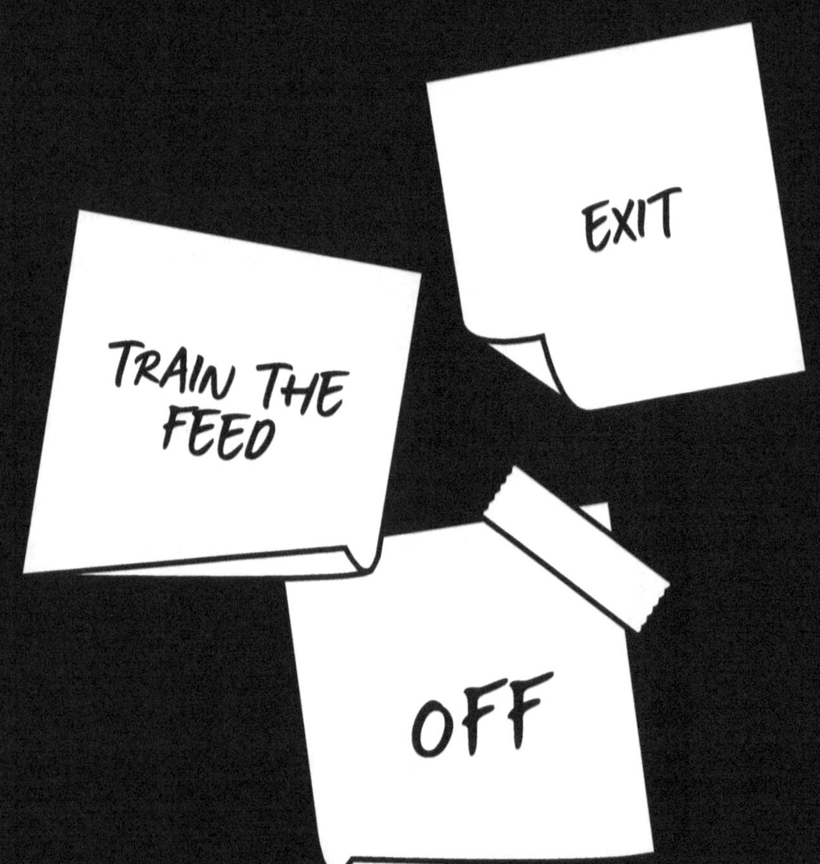
EXIT
TRAIN THE FEED
OFF

GETTING OUT

Getting out of the trap of widespread engagement by creating contents that many people don't like that much, in order to come up with something that fewer people will enjoy, but for longer than just the time for a scroll.

Getting out, as users, of the vicious circle of the algorithm making choices for us and annoying us. We should take responsibility for our decisions by learning to train the system, for example through resets made every two or three months, at least until we have the super social media we dream of. Basically, we should try to polish our feeds, even deciding to stop following people who are now estranged from us.

Getting out of the hive life, and out of the customer-centred trap that has made us hysterical rats chasing time and money, success and fame. Whenever possible, getting out of those situations that are bad for us, like quitting a job that makes us depressed, or giving up one or more clients that treat us like slaves.

And finding at least some form of outlet, when the situation is not yet critical, reminding ourselves that chronic stress is mightier than the pen, which was once said to be mightier than the sword.

Getting out of our tiny houses and of social media whenever we can so as to watch the world outside, let our eyes rest, and meet people face-to-face and not online.
And, while we are with them, we should keep our devices switched off or buy a phone that our grandparents would like, those with nothing to scroll through, to be clear.

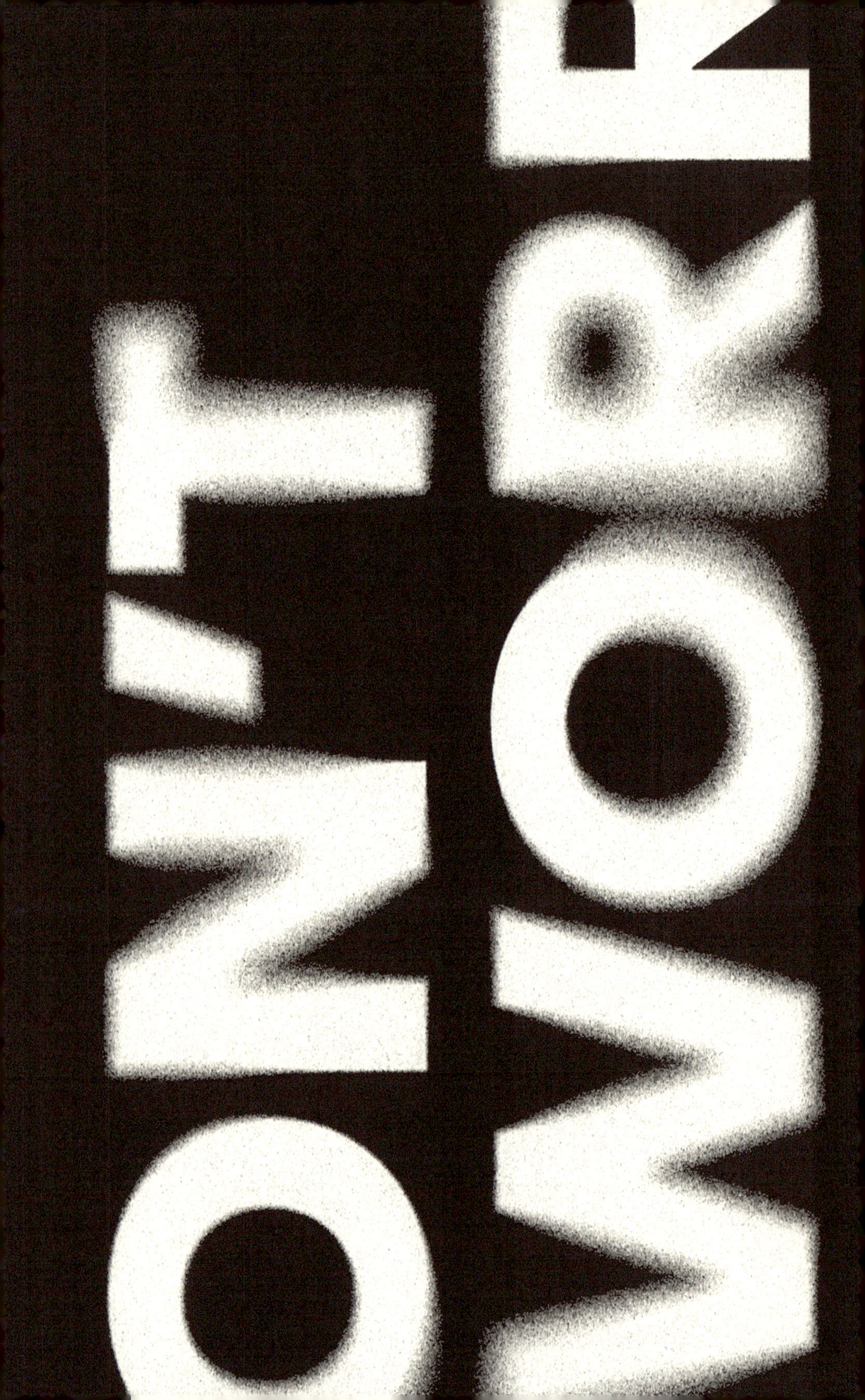

DON'T WORRY
ABOUT THE FUTURE

Big Kahuna

In an hotel room, three vendors are waiting for a convention to begin. Kevin Spacey and Danny De Vito are two veterans of trade, the first is cynical, the second bored and pissed off, while Peter Facinelli is an under-30 novice. The company they work for is in bad shape, but on the horizon, or maybe already in the hotel lobby, there is a big customer - the Big Kahuna - that could increase the turnover alone.

Kammerspiel

While waiting for the convention to start, the three are speaking by staging a "kammerspiel"* that ends with a voice-over, whose words** have become legendary.

When the film was released in American cinemas, it was 1999, the year in which the young Mario was also opening his first startup, the same Mario who now, much less young, chooses to share ten of them.

Don't worry about the future.

Or worry,

but know that worrying
        is as effective
           as trying to solve
     an algebra equation
by chewing bubble gum.

---

*   'Kammerspiel' - chamber + play

**   The words of the voice come from an article by Mary Schmich, journalist of the Chicago Tribune, published back in 1997, three years before the film, entitled "Advice, like youth, probably just wasted on the young", also known as Wear Sunscreen.

1.Don't worry about the future. Or worry, but know that worrying is as effective as trying to solve an algebra equation by chewing bubble gum.

2. Every day, do one thing that scares you. Sing.

☑ *Il Caffettino counts, doesn't it?*

3.Keep all the old love letters, throw away the old bank statements.

☑ *But if you live in Italy,*
   keep them all for ten years.

4.Relax.

5. Don't feel guilty if you don't know what you want to do with your life. The most interesting people I know, at twenty-two years old didn't know what to do with their life. The most interesting forty-year-olds I know, still don't know.

☐ *Excuse me, Professor Galimberti,*
   but then there is hope....

don't

6. Maybe you will get married or maybe not. Maybe you will have children or maybe not. Maybe you will get divorced at the age of forty. Maybe you will dance with her at your seventy-fifth wedding anniversary. Either way, don't congratulate yourself too much, but don't beat yourself up either. Your choices are bets. Like everyone else's.

☑ *A son I did have. His name is Francis, he was born in 2020, and before he turns three years old has already taught me that certain clientele dressed as Big Kahuna need to be dropped.*

7. Realize that friends come and go. But some, the most valuable, will remain.

☑ *I take this opportunity to say. Ale the Fer from Holland (lucky him), Marco from Arluno (lucky us), Ivo with our impossible challenges, Igor with titanic feats and a few others who never ever left.*

8. Get busy bridging geographic distances and lifestyles, because the older you get, the more you need the people you knew when you were young.

☑ *See above.*

9. Live in New York for a while, but leave it before it hardens you. Live in California for a while, too, but leave it before it softens you.

☑ *Done (California was my home for a few months in 2006)*

Be cautious about taking advice, but be patient with those who dispense it. Advice is a form of nostalgia. Dispensing it is a way of dredging up the past from oblivion, cleaning it up, paint over the ugliest parts and recycle it for more than it's worth.

But I'll take the advice...

just this once.

CREDITS

If this book has reached those who are reading it, it is because social media is not over. What is over - GAME OVER - is the era in which we used to tell ourselves that they could give everything to everyone with no problem. This end, just as Winston (Churchill, not Castaway's ball) said, is the beginning of another one where we take responsibility for the choices we make.

The end and the beginning of social media came from the contributions of many people, just like this little book, whose 35,000 words, roughly speaking, come from various suggestions that I will now ask you to imagine as they scroll, in order of appearance:

Valentina Sala

Francesco Moroni

Fabrizio, Lara, Gloria, Walter, the people who follow my podcasts and events, and the readers of Startup by M.

Mark Fisher

Shoshana Zuboff

Gavin Mueller

Andy Grove

Winston Churchill

My friend from Berlin

Davide Wallace Wells

Luca Tomassini

Douglas Adams

Ellis Hamburger

Ian Bogost

Ivan Pavlov

Matteo Flora

Albert Einstein

Hippocrates of Kos

Galen of Pergamon

Sebastian Kneipp

Ludwig Feuerbach

Giancarlo Orsini

Pink Floyd

Germano Lanzoni

Martin Wolf

Woody Allen

Alvin Toffler

Philip Kotler

Martin Moore

Jaron Lanier

Iron Maiden

Jared Diamond

Niccolò, Matteo and Marco Polo

Cristoforo Colombo

Guglielmo Marconi

Sigmund Freud

Fabri Fibra

Giuseppe Ortoleva
Furio Jesi
Wu-Ming foundation
Vikas Swarup
Narciso
Chiara Ferragni
Alessandro Barbero
Francesco Fratto
Barbascura X
Alessandro Masala
Marina Cuollo
Anthony Robbins
Roberto Re
Livio Sgarbi
Giovanna D'Alessio
Robert Suttone Jeffrey Pfeffer
Marco Montemagno
Satoshi Nakamoto

William Shakespeare
Clifton Meador
Fantozzi
Irvine Welsh
Thomas Piketty
Henry Ford
Checco Zalone
Lisa Feldman Barrett
Oliver Burkeman
Ray Kurzweil
Jerry Kaplan
Geoffrey Hinton
Nick Bostrom
Pedro Domingos
Socrate
Umberto Galimberti
Mary Schmich
Irvine Welsh

236

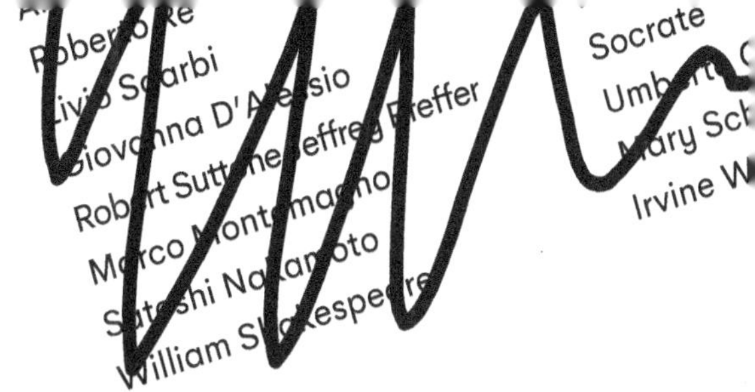

The suggestions mentioned above have come to me both over the years as well as recently, helping me to put the words you are reading on the page, but in order to take the form you see, they have involved various forces, without which, nothingness.

Mario Moroni
 Direction and screenplay

Youcanprint
 Production company that helped me in this experiment. They describe themselves as 'self-publishing with human support'; in my opinion, Donato and co. are much more than that.
Well done!

Roberta Giulia Amidani
 Sound and speech engineering, costumes, set design, and final cleaning: fundamental for the editing part afterwards, and for the construction part beforehand.

Simone Checchia and Giorgia de Giambattista from Blueorange®, who, besides creating the cover, help me in my "creative dispersions" of the series "this is punk, we have to do it!"
 Special effects/graphics

... and in random order
according to the latest WhatsApp messages received today :)

Alessandro Best *(thank you for Fisher, you're a game changer!)*, Alessandro Cialli *(we will always advance)*, Francesca Bellotto *(we are Lucca)*, Fabio Balossi *(don't get mad)*, Erminia Torre *(thank you for your patience)*, Gabriele Capra *(come on and cheer up!)*, Lorenzo Ferrara *(the social Florence boss)*, Michele Franzese *(I told you so, but display?)*, Cristina Pontiggia *(the month of boh)*, Ariele Frizzante *(the voice)*, Massimo Temporelli *(Guglielmo Marconi)*, Renato Franchi *(what a player)*, Alessandro Vercellotti *(but what does the guarantor say?)*, Angie *(Mario but better, feminine)*, Heidi Iuliano *(my name is Mario)*, Paolo Cavagnini *(can you make me thinner?)*, Rudy Bandiera *(we have to grill)*, Rossella Pivanti *(branded what's coming)*, Giuseppe Bellini *(the lawyer)*, Riccardo Scandellari *(the guiding light)*, Enrico Battistelli *(the talents of Pesaro)*, Ettore Allegretti *(how do we play it best?)*, Riccardo Esposito *(but does it work on google?)*, Gabriele Rapino *(we are 2 incredible dads)*, Daniele Barbone *(see you on New Year's Eve, very quickly)*, and to all the others who have etched their notes and/or symphonies on this book as well.

The whole community, in particular THANK YOU to "Il Caffettino" / Patreon Club that supports me every month with donations, suggestions and stimulating discussions

The whole co

particular THANK

Caffettino" / P

that supports me

with donations

NO EXCUSES

HELLO MARK,
SO WHAT HAVE YOU BEEN UP TO IN THESE TWENTY YEARS?

– Hey Mark

– So, what've you been up to these last twenty years?

...

– In these twenty years?
With these words, the official trailer for Trainspotting 2 kicks off, the movie based on two novels[*] by Irvine Welsh, directed by Danny Boyle[**] and written by John Hodge. As Trainspotting 2 is my favourite film, after the credits, here's the final monologue.

Choose life

Choose Facebook, Twitter, Instagram

and hope that someone, somewhere, cares

Choose to look for old lovers, wishing you had acted differently

And choose to watch history repeat itself

Choose your future

Choose reality shows, getting dragged, and porn

Choose a zero-hour contract, a two-hour commute

And the same for your kids, and ease the pain with an unknown dose of an unknown drug made in someone's kitchen

And then... take a deep breath

You are addicts

Then get high

But with something else

Choose the people you love

Choose the future

Choose life.

---

[*] The two novels are "Trainspotting" and "Porno".

[**] Danny Boyle is also the director of Slumdog Millionaire, from 2008, based on the novel "Q&A" by Vikas Swarup.

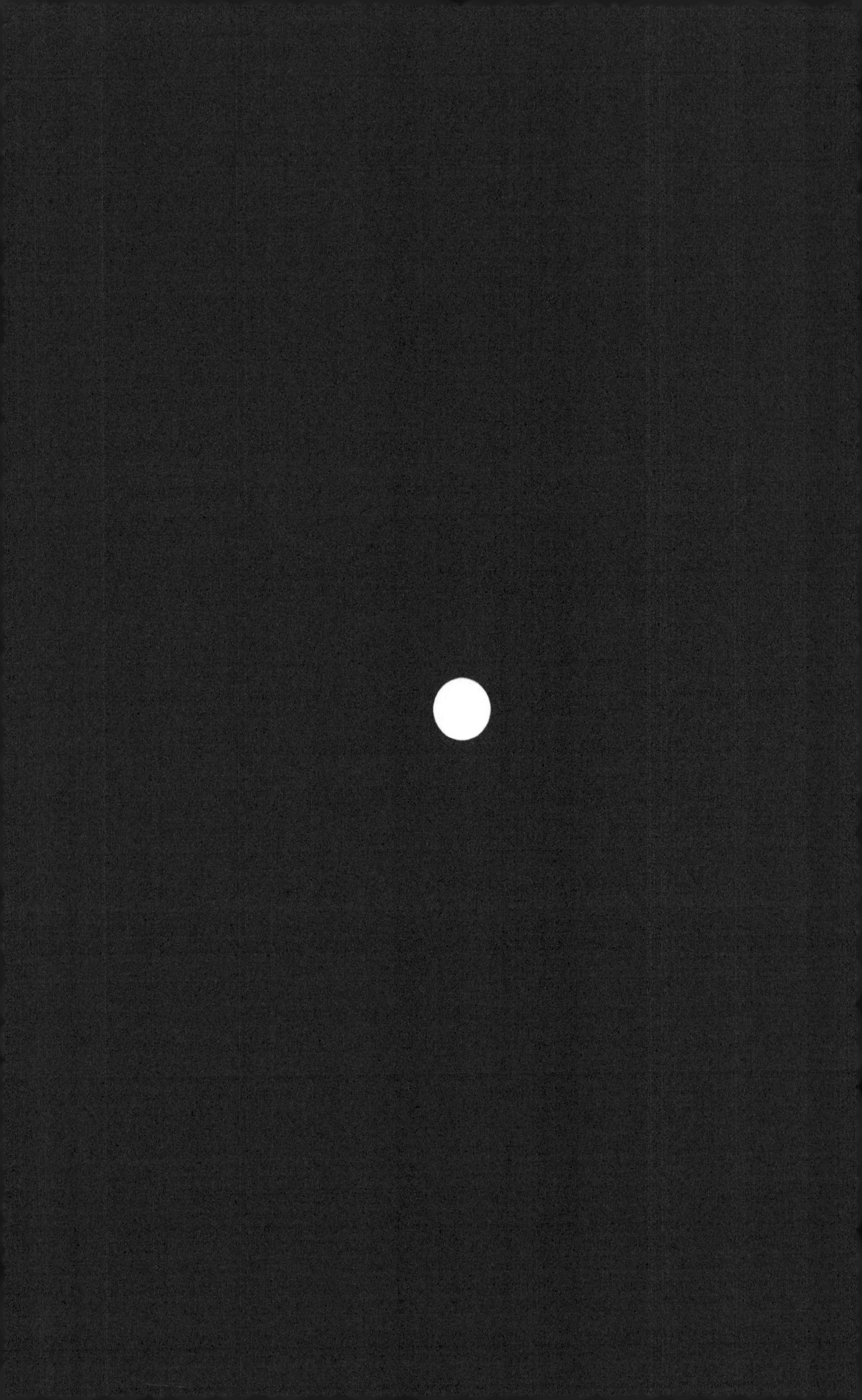

THE END

We depend on the myths that we have made up, the language we use, the food we eat and the planet we ignore. We depend on the comparison with the others and on the identity we would like to have. We depend on the opinion of the others. We depend on money, progress and devices. We depend on the environment we have shaped and sold.

And so, it's true, we are all a bit toxic. There is a countdown and there are the drums of the trolls.

The end of social media and the beginning of the artificial intelligence era, which is threatening our world, is just a moment where we will be forced to face our responsibilities with the aim of being human, and therefore - since we are all a bit toxic – to choose new addictions.

Six months after the first edition of this podcast-book, social media have already some paid options. Micro communities are catching on. The former Twitter, now X, has lost 25 billion in value passing from 44 billion to 19 billion. Eight jobs out of ten are intended to be revolutionised by AI.

As I am writing this update, I can already see 2024 as the definitive turning point, the year zero for policy choices on social media, technology, progress and the related regulations/liberalisations.

I don't want to make prophecies. At least not here.

No matter what happens, I repeat that the end of social media and the beginning of the artificial intelligence era, which is threating our world, is just a moment where we will be forced to face our responsibilities with the aim of being human, and therefore – since we are all a bit toxic – to choose new addictions.

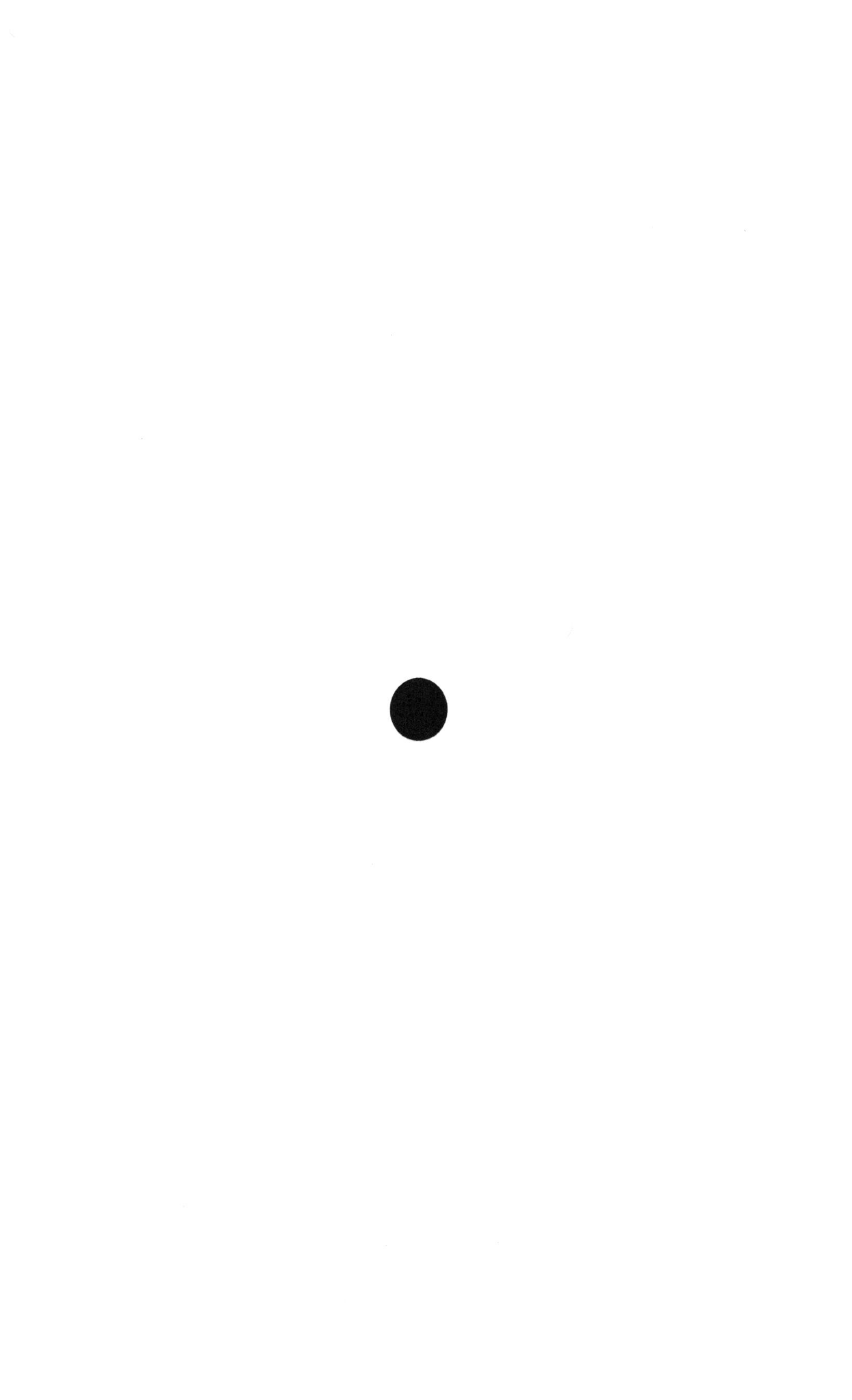

SOURCES

1 "The engagement economy: how gamification is reshaping business", Doug Palmer, Steve Lunceford e Aaron J. Patton https://www.digital4.biz/marketing/engagement-economy-connected-customer-marketing-intelligence/

2 https://www.neroeditions.com/product/tecnoluddismo/

3 S. ZUBOFF SAID IT IN 2013, THE AGE OF SURVAIVAL CAPITALISM

4 https://www.engage.it/rubrica/engagement-economy-continua-e-data-driven.aspx
https://www.digital4.biz/marketing/engagement-economy-connected-customer-marketing-intelligence/

5 Luca Tomassini, il salto quantico, LUISS, 2020

6 https://acleddata.com/#/dashboard

7 https://www.huffingtonpost.it/dossier/fintech/2022/11/20/news/crisi_social-10728620/

8 ELLIS HAMBURGER WAS A REPORTER AT THE VERGE, THAN HE QUITTED TO GO IN SNAPCHAT. SEVEN YEARS LATER, HE STARTED WORKINF FOR THE BROWSER COMPANY https://www.theverge.com/2023/4/18/23672769/social-media-inevitable-death-monetization-growth-hacks

9 The Age of Social Media Is Ending - It never should have begun. By Ian Bogost https://www.theatlantic.com/technology/archive/2022/11/twitter-facebook-social-media-decline/672074/

10 https://www.wired.it/article/x-a-pagamento-microabbonamento/

11 https://www.businessinsider.com/elon-musk-considering-taking-twitter-x-out-of-europe-dsa-2023-10?r=US&IR=T

12 https://www.euractiv.com/section/platforms/news/musk-considers-removing-x-platform-from-europe-over-eu-law/

13 https://www.ilsole24ore.com/art/arrivano-facebook-e-instagram-pagamento-ecco-quanto-costano-e-come-funzionano-AFTO1oRB

14 https://www.agi.it/estero/news/2023-10-21/twitter-x-fake-news-elon-musk-utenti-premium-23574983/

15 Francesco Fratto, "Intestino senza pensieri", Sperling & Kupfer

16 (Arthur Wallace Pickard-Cambridge e Donald William Lucas, "Dizionario di antichità classiche", Edizioni San Paolo, Cinisello Balsamo, 1995, pp. 2123-4)

17 https://www.ministeroturismo.gov.it/italia-open-to-meraviglia/

18 https://www.uominiedonnecomunicazione.com/cannes-lions-2010-sfida-tra-creativi/

19 https://www.repubblica.it/tecnologia/2010/06/23/news/intervista_a_zuckerberg-5098864/

20 https://www.ilpost.it/2011/11/23/i-gradi-di-separazione-su-facebook/

21 https://www.repubblica.it/economia/rapporti/obiettivo-capitale/mercati/2022/10/04/news/ogni_5_secondi_in_italia_una_coppia_si_separa_tempi_lunghi_e_costi_fino_a_60mila_euro_per_divorziare-368548854/

22 https://www.ansa.it/canale_lifestyle/notizie/societa_diritti/2019/04/08/ondata-divorzi-nel-mondo-785-entro-2030-e-calo-figli.-cambia-tutto-dalle-case-alla-sanita_03cdf953-dbbe-4564-a8be-8bb11e5a7eaa.html

23 https://luce.lanazione.it/economia/finche-divorzio-non-ci-separi-meglio-soli-che-sposati-in-italia-e-piu-che-un-modo-di-dire/

24 https://zinginstruments.com/songs-about-money/

25 https://www.ilpost.it/2019/09/22/democrazia-capitalismo-martin-wolf/

26 https://www.eiu.com/n/democracy-index-2021-less-than-half-the-world-lives-in-a-democracy/

27 https://www.youtrend.it/2022/03/01/quanti-e-quali-stati-possono-essere-definiti-democrazie/

28 People versus Tech (Bartlett, 2018)

29 "Democracy Hacked - Political Turmoil and Information Warfare in the Digital Age" - Martin Moore, Oneworld Publications, 2018

30 Arthur Wallace Pickard-Cambridge e Donald William Lucas, Dizionario di antichità classiche, Edizioni San Paolo, Cinisello Balsamo, 1995, pp. 2123-4

31 Quoted by Jan-Werner Müller - Professor of Social Sciences and Politics at Princeton University where he founded and directs the Project in the History of Political Thought, author of numerous publications, including: "What is Populism?" (Egea 2023), "Democracy Rules" (Penguin 2021) and "Contesting Democracy. Political Ideas in Twentieth Century Europe" (Yale University Press 2011) - «CBS Weekend News», Internet Archive, May 7, 2016, available online

32 https://acleddata.com/#/dashboard

33 https://www.ansa.it/sito/notizie/topnews/2023/10/29/ministero-hamas-oltre-8.000-morti-nella-striscia-di-gaza_eb930054-bdd4-47ac-8ad4-082a0e9ea133.html

34 https://edition.cnn.com/middleeast/live-news/israel-hamas-war-gaza-10-10-23/h_0be6fd543c16ccd27f75f1448c18537

35 https://tg24.sky.it/mondo/2023/02/23/guerra-ucraina-numeri-social-zelensky

36   https://www.ilmessaggero.it/mondo/guerra_ucraina_documenti_segreti_nato_usa_piano_guerra_russia_cosa_sappiamo-7332758.html

37 https://www.wumingfoundation.com/giap/2018/01/mito/

38 Barthes, quoted by Enrico Manera, su https://www.wumingfoundation.com/giap/2018/01/mito/

39 https://italianluxuryasset.com/who-is-chiara-ferragni-why-is-she-globally-famous/

41 https://www.forbes.com/profile/chiara-ferragni/

42 https://www.contra-ataque.it/2023/02/07/chiara-ferragni-chi-e.html

43   Luigi Mascheroni,   Il Giornale,   https://www.ilgiornale.it/news/politica/super-manager-nulla-che-s-presa-tutto-anche-rai-2113089.html

44 https://www.cattolicanews.it/siamo-tutti-influencers

45 https://medium.com/the-partnered-pen/i-asked-chatgpt-how-to-earn-1000-online-it-was-hilarious-33189ab03f60

46 https://www.vice.com/it/article/yvaqgg/guru-non--una-parolaccia-a9n3

48   https://www.econopoly.ilsole24ore.com/2022/12/09/ftx-altruismo-efficace/#:~:text=Il%20fallimento%20di%20FTX%2C%20causato,semplicemente%20una%20truffa%20ben%20mascherata

49 https://www.wired.it/article/ftx-crollo-bahamas-crisi/

50   https://www.imf.org/en/Publications/fandd/issues/2022/09/Point-of-View-the-superficial-allure-of-crypto-Hilary-Allen

51 According to the University of Cambridge's Bitcoin Electricity Consumption Index

52 https://energiaoltre.it/perche-limpronta-carbonica-dei-bitcoin-ha-raggiunto-il-massimo-storico/

53 https://www.internazionale.it/notizie/romaric-godin/2022/05/24/criptovalute-crollo-capitalismo

54 Shoshana Zuboff, "Il capitalismo della sorveglianza", pag. 115

55 Four Thousand Weeks: Time Management for MortalsFour Thousand Weeks: Time Management for Mortal, 2021

56 Shoshana Zuboff, "Il capitalismo della sorveglianza", pag. 3

57 https://www.ilsole24ore.com/art/la-casa-diventa-sempre-piu-piccola-AETKik7D

58   https://www.bloomberg.com/news/articles/2023-04-04/a-fifth-of-1-5-million-japanese-holed-up-at-home-blame-covid

59 Jerry Kaplan, "Le persone non servono, lavoro e ricchezza nell'epoca dell'intelligenza artificiale" LUISS, 2016

60 "Geoffrey Hinton tells us why he's now scared of the tech he helped build", MIT Technology Review, maggio 2023 https://www.technologyreview.com/2023/05/02/1072528/geoffrey-hinton-google-why-scared-ai/

61 https://www.technologyreview.com/2023/05/02/1072528/geoffrey-hinton-google-why-scared-ai/

62 https://www.bbc.com/news/technology-65139406

63 Jerry Kaplan, Le persone non servono, lavoro e intelligenza nell'epoca dell'intelligenza artificiale, LUISS, 2016.

64 https://www.businessoffashion.com/articles/technology/hm-group-is-using-ai/

65   https://www.latimes.com/entertainment-arts/business/story/2023-10-20/authors-ai-lawsuits-douglas-preston-george-rr-martin-michael-connelly

66 https://laist.com/brief/news/arts-and-entertainment/thousands-of-authors-urge-ai-companies-to-stop-using-work-without-permission

67   https://learningenglish.voanews.com/a/publishers-worry-over-google-s-new-ai-search-tool-/7322496.html

68   https://www.wired.it/article/giuliano-amato-commissione-algoritmi-intelligenza-artificiale-barachini-meloni/#:~:text=Giuliano%20Amato%20presiede%20un%20comitato%20su%20intelligenza%20artificiale%20ed%20editoria,-Il%20costituzionalista%2085enne&text=Il%20governo%20Meloni%20ha%20affidato,'editoria%2C%20ribattezzata%20commissione%20algoritmi.

69   https://www.technologyreview.com/2023/10/23/1082189/data-poisoning-artists-fight-generative-ai/

70 https://open.spotify.com/episode/1OYwWdhbebL4mcwApGsOc1?si=615e1717542c44c0

71 https://www.linkedin.com/feed/update/urn:li:activity:7131929346503585792/

72 https://www.repubblica.it/tecnologia/2023/03/10/news/meta_instagram_app_twitter-391443756/

73 https://wisesociety.it/incontri/umberto-galimberti-ecco-perche-non-possiamo-fare-la-rivoluzione/